Endorsements

"If you are reading this, either you are a member of the club you never wanted to join—widowhood—or perhaps you are a friend or family of a widow. If life feels sad, confusing, disappointing, or even filled with a swirling mix of emotions, you are in the right place to gain the hope, help, and healing you long for! Your heart is in good hands! These seasoned widows, including author, editor, and publisher, Virginia Grounds, along with others have penned a treasure trove of encouragement, enrichment, and inspiration straight from God's heart to your own heart. You can move forward, one step at a time, with the guidance of God and the rich wisdom of the plethora of widows who know the path you are walking. This book is a cross between coffee with best friends and a daily Bible study with the Creator God who can and will create a path forward for you."

—Pam Farrel
Author of more than sixty books, including bestselling
Men Are Like Waffles, Women Are Like Spaghetti and
Discovering Hope in the Psalms:
A Creative Bible Study Experience
Co-Director of Love-Wise.com

"*W.I.N.G.S.: Hope for Widows in New Growth Seasons* is a touching and essential guide for those navigating the heart-wrenching journey of widowhood. Through a compassionate lens, this book skillfully combines biblical prophecy and practical advice to provide hope for widows. The exploration of 'Widow Brain' is enlightening, offering much-needed clarity and understanding about the emotional and cognitive impacts of profound loss. Each page is a gentle reminder that through faith and the healing power of God's promises, renewal and growth are not just possible but promised.

W.I.N.G.S illuminates the path to healing and hope with the warmth of God's love."

—Susan Neal RN, MBA, MHS
Author of *12 Ways to Age Gracefully*

"Filled with personal stories, biblical encouragement, and tips for how to move forward, *W.I.N.G.S.* provides help and hope as you pursue what God holds for your future."

—Katie Orr
Author, Speaker, and Director of the Bible Study Hub

"I know those reading the words in this book will be inspired to continue to live with intentionality and purpose. I have also walked the journey of being a widow and am so thankful for God's provision and protection as I learned to walk on a different path. The timing is different for us all but be encouraged—GOD is walking with you every STEP of the way. This book shares that in a transparent way."

—Sondra Saunders
Pastoral care at Prestonwood Baptist Church, Plano, Texas

"In the Message of Hope behind each chapter, Virginia Grounds tenderly weaves together words of wisdom, touching stories of widows, and actionable steps to help you find solace and renewed purpose in the face of loss. This compassionate guide offers biblical guidance and practical tools for those seeking hope and healing. A must-read for anyone navigating the complexities of grief."

—Dee Humphrey
Bible Teacher, Speaker, and Director of Women's Ministry, FBC
Grove, Oklahoma

"This book, *W.I.N.G.S.: Hope for Widows in New Growth Seasons,* answers many of the questions widows may be experiencing. It is well written in a form that is easy to read and understand. Thank you, my friend, for writing a book to help widows wondering, 'What now?'"

—Iva Nell (Ivy) Caselman
WINGS Widows Group Leader, FBC Grove, Oklahoma

W.I.N.G.S.

Hope for Widows in New Growth Seasons

But you who fear my name,
The sun of righteousness shall rise
With healing in its wings…
Malachi 4:2a (ESV)

Wings: *A poetic image of the rays of sun bringing healing*
to all who come under its influence.
In Malachi, it is a prophecy fulfilled in Jesus.

Hope: *Confident expectation of good.*

Virginia Grounds

With Contributing Authors

Published by Breakthrough Christian Publishing
www.breakthroughchristianpublishing.com

ISBN: 979-8-9907557-8-9 Paperback
ISBN: 979-8-9907557-9-6 Ebook

Library of Congress Control Number: 1-14687100231

Published in the United States of America

Contents

Note: The "Tips for Living Forward" at the end of each chapter are provided by Jenny Leavitt. The "Message of Hope" entries are by Virginia Grounds.

Preface

What Is Widow Brain?

People refer to the feeling of disconnect and fogginess after the loss of a spouse as "Widow Brain." This was an unfamiliar term for me, but I am relieved to know there was a reason for what I, and many others, experienced as recent widows. It is believed that the Widow Brain acts as a coping mechanism to shield itself from excruciating pain and grief. Knowing there is a name for the symptoms helps those who have experienced the loss of their loved one to know their response is normal. We may think we are abnormal because the symptoms can last from two months to one year or longer. The more we deny grief, the longer the Widow Brain will last.

Some stages of grief are denial, anger, depression, and acceptance. We may deny our grief to surface, but still have a foggy brain. We may get angry at our spouse for leaving us, or at God for taking them, then fail to remember the source of our anger. If we do not address the anger, bitterness will become a way of life. The Widow Brain will exist whether or not we give in to grief. It is our body's response to loss, trauma, and unexpected tragedy.

Widow Brain Symptoms[1]

- Forgetfulness
- Extreme Sadness
- Brain Fog

1   Trust&Will. "What Is 'Widow Brain' after the Death of a Spouse?" Trust&Will.com, 2025. https://trustandwill.com/learn/widow-brain

- Irritability
- Fatigue or Exhaustion
- Numbness
- Nausea

My brain has always been sharp in remembering things, but in that first year, I noticed I could not remember names and important information. Sadness was deep and no matter what I did, I could not rise above it. The smallest thing would set me off. The fogginess was affecting my work and relationships. I experienced every single symptom. What a relief to discover that it is not just me.

Praise God that with time and healing, we can press on in a new beginning with hope for our future. God knows the grief and struggle we have. He knows the pain and mental fog that keeps us in isolation. He heals the brokenhearted and has an answer for what is next for us as we navigate life without our mate.

We can endure by holding onto God and his Word, letting time pass while nurturing hope for what lies ahead. We will never forget our loved one, but with time, we will rise above the grief and pain to hope again. Looking forward instead of backward is a start to the healing process.

As you read the stories written by widows, keep in mind they have been in their new season longer than a year. If you are in your first year, be encouraged by their progress, but don't be discouraged if you are not there emotionally yet. Know that we have all experienced an unwanted new beginning.

– Virginia

Introduction

Spread Your Wings

Hope for Widows in New Growth Seasons

But for you who fear my name,
The sun of righteousness shall rise
With healing in its wings...

Malachi 4:2a (ESV)

What is next for me? This might be a question you've thought about. But life is not over for a widow, even though it may seem that way for a while. We are no longer a couple, but don't feel single. In fact, we may still feel married yet alone. How can we move forward productively? The answer is to stay connected to God through his Word and prayer.

Moving forward following the loss of a loved one, especially your husband, is difficult. We grieve at a different pace, and moving forward is not going to be the same for us as it is for others. We all experience grief stages, but God guides us to move forward when the time is right. He desires us to receive healing from our tears and sorrow without letting go of our best memories as he guides us towards a fulfilling life in this new widowhood season.

Authors who have suffered the loss of their husbands contributed to this book. Each one shares their story of loss to reveal that, even though the loss is difficult, there is a way to live future-focused. We can learn from one another, each in our unique way.

Our stories aim to encourage you with the way God works in our lives as widows, not to remind you of grief or drag you into despair. As he has done for others, he can do for you. He may urge you toward an unexpected new beginning and an opportunity to grow in your relationship with him as well as develop new friendships. But one thing is certain. He is with us to see us through an uncertain time following our loss.

Between the stories, I have written Messages of Hope with Bible study questions for encouragement as we enter this new season. Focused on the future, hope banishes fear of what is to come. Our hope is not an emotion, but a divine attribute of God. He is our hope. We can have faith in the promising future he has for us. He gives us the courage to face tomorrow. We can learn from Jesus's actions and message to the disciples as he prepared them for his departure and their grief. He knew they would grieve and gave them the tools to cope and live forward. The Bible study questions are simply to direct our focus to Jesus. That is what helped me through my grief, and I pray it will help you to focus on him as well. These questions are optional.

I suggest reading one chapter and working through one Message of Hope per day, rather than trying to read them all at once. Moving forward takes time. Recovery doesn't happen all at once. Therefore, reading the entire book at once will not accomplish its purpose for you.

This means in our sorrow, one step forward is enough to get us through the day. We can have confidence knowing God has gone before us into tomorrow. He finds a way for us when there appears to be none.

While reading, observe how each woman progressed. The book's goal is to help you apply any of these steps to press on to the future God has for you. When you find a helpful tip, write it in a journal as a personal reminder, or underline it in this book.

Apply the end-of-chapter **"Tips for Living Forward"** suggestions provided by Jenny Leavitt.

Take heart, dear friend. You are loved and prayed for.

– Virginia

And the king said to her,
"What is your trouble?"
She answered,
"Alas, I am a widow;
my husband is dead."

2 Sam. 14:5 (ESV)

Chapter 1

A Greater Love

Virginia Grounds

We love because he first loved us.

1 John 4:19 (ESV)

As we stood at the altar, we repeated wedding vows with stars in our eyes and love in our hearts. We were so in love that saying, "For better or worse, for richer or poorer, in sickness and in health, till death do us part," were simply words we spoke. Love blinded us to the true meaning of "in sickness and in health." Forty-five years later, we understood the meaning all too well.

As widows, we know the meaning behind these words and understand why they are in wedding vows. A vow is serious and something to be taken with the full intent of following through. The "worse, poorer, sickness, and death" are all part of a marriage, just as the better things are. Long marriages go through everything. The vows are to prepare us for it.

Yet, through hard experiences, there is still love. Love deepens with years as we hold on to Jesus and each other. It takes the greater love of Jesus flowing from him through us to comfort the one who is ill and dying. It is his love that gives us the ability to do things for them that are beyond our human ability—things we couldn't fathom as we stood at the altar on our wedding day.

Jesus is the one who loves without condition and more than we can comprehend. He passes this love through us into the lives of those we care for. There is no greater love than this. Love prevails when caring for a sick spouse, even in frustrating, exhausting, angry, or resentful moments. And because of his greater love, we have greater love to give to make our loved one's transition easier.

If you are reading this book, it may mean your caregiving days are over. The time of widowhood has begun. My heart grieves with you. Be encouraged. There is hope for your future because God gives new mercies of compassion each morning. Every day is a new beginning.

Memories of greater love will remain, and even though we grieve because of the loss, we can recover because of the love.

We love because he first loved us.

Tips for Living Forward

Reflect on the legacy of your marriage and lean on the promise of life in Christ to find hope and peace.

Message of Hope – 1

Preparation for Departure

Now before the feast of the Passover
when Jesus knew that his hour had come
to depart out of this world to the Father,
having loved his own who were in the world,
he loved them to the end.

John 13:1 (ESV)

"I need a haircut," my husband said as he lay in his hospice bed. So, I gave him a haircut and he looked so good. He then asked me to cut his toenails. That was the first time he had ever asked me to do that, so I was surprised. Confession—I didn't really want to do it, and didn't understand why he wanted it. I gathered the supplies I would need, washed his feet, trimmed the nails, and massaged his feet with lotion. He then wanted to know when his aide was coming to give him a bath. "Tomorrow," I replied. Then he patted his bed and said, "Sit down for a minute. I want to talk to you." The day after his bath, he lost his ability to speak, and the day after that, Jesus took him home.

It wasn't until after that I realized he wanted to look his best for meeting Jesus face to face and was preparing himself and me for his departure. Not only did he want to look his best, but he also wanted to assure me of his love. Somehow he knew he would be gone in a few days, but I did not.

This experience has given me a new understanding of how the disciples could not believe Jesus would leave them. But Jesus was preparing them for his departure by giving instruction for how to live in a way that grief would not consume them.

Read John 13:1–11. What was the occasion according to verse 1?

What did Jesus do when he rose from supper?

What was Jesus's answer to Peter's question according to verses 6–7?

What do you think Jesus meant when he said, "If I do not wash you, you have no share with me"?

Peter was like a child who does not understand why they need to be clean and therefore doesn't want a bath. But Jesus taught in parables, examples, and illustrations symbolizing another meaning. Such was the case here. The foot-washing symbolized the cleansing that is needed to take away our sin. If the cleansing of sin did not take place, he was letting Peter know his access to God would be hindered.

> **Look back at verse 1, the last two phrases. Who did Jesus love and for how long?**

This lesson began with love. **Jesus prepared the disciples for his departure because of his love for them**. It was a forever love. His response to Peter was to help him understand the reason for Jesus coming into the world. It is because God loved the world so much that he sent his Son, Jesus, so we would be cleansed of our sin and know him in a personal way (see John 3:16).

The physical presence of our husband's love is no longer with us but our love for them is. Does the forever love of God give you the comfort of his presence in your grief? God is love and his love is everlasting for you.

For the mountains may depart
And the hills be removed,
But my steadfast love shall not depart from you...
Isaiah 54:10a (ESV)

All the widows
stood beside him weeping
And showing tunics and
other garments
that Dorcas made while
she was with them.

Acts 9:39 (ESV)

Chapter 2

A New Beginning

Virginia Grounds

Behold, I will do something new,
Now it will spring forth;
Will you not be aware of it?
I will even make a roadway in the wilderness,
Rivers in the desert.

Isaiah 43:19 (NASB95)

New beginnings can be exciting when they involve something we love. In fact, each new day is a new beginning. When God gives a new opportunity, we can find a sense of fulfillment in following where he leads. But there is a new beginning that is not wanted by most women. It is the beginning of widowhood. It is a time in life when dramatic changes come, especially for those who have been married for a long time.

The time after a loss can feel like an endless wilderness for a widow. A dry, barren, lonely desert without hope. But God has promised new beginnings. He makes a way when we may think there is not one. God is faithful to do what he says.

Having lost my spouse, I empathize with the grief and sense of loss. But as a believer, I also understand the comfort and healing that comes from our Savior, Jesus Christ. Many others prayed for me during the first months after my husband died, and I couldn't have navigated my grief without their support. But God is so faithful to provide support and encouragement from lifelong friends when we need it the most. And knowing we have the spirit of God who intercedes for us when we cannot pray for ourselves is comforting.

And yet, there is a reality to face. The first time I had to write the word "widow" on a form was when it became real to me. I was now alone. As widows, the temptation to isolate ourselves is normal, but not wise. Loneliness is a common feeling and, if not addressed, we will wallow in grief. And yes, God gives us the grief process to guide us toward healing. But he does not want us to get stuck there. He encourages us to move forward, learning a new way of living without our loved one.

In that moment, our best course of action is to turn to Jesus, the greatest friend we could ever ask for. He can give us peace in our situation that no other can. It is then we can accept our new beginning. Our marriage was a dedicated time in our lives. But now we enter a season of new beginnings. Remember, God still has plans for us. There is something around the bend just waiting for us to get there. A fulfilling and productive life can lead us to experience joy once more. It will be different, but we have not lost our identity. We are still daughters of the King.

After a year of grief, I sensed a stirring in my heart to get back to ministry. Yet, I ignored the nudging for several months. However, when I finally followed God's direction, unexpected doors to ministry opened, opportunities I wouldn't have pursued if he hadn't presented them to me. It only took four days from the time I let go of what God was asking of me and the time a new door opened. My lesson learned from the experience is to listen and pay attention to those prompts from the Lord and trust him for the rest. He loves and cares for widows and makes a way for us according to our need. We can trust him. He is our hope.

Tips for Living Forward

Embrace new beginnings by surrendering your plans to God's will. Isaiah 43:19 reminds us that God is always doing a new thing. Pray for his guidance to see opportunities for growth, healing, and purpose.

Message of Hope – 2

Preparation by Example

*When he had washed their feet and put on his outer garments
and resumed his place, he said to them,
"Do you understand what I have done to you?"*

John 13:12 (ESV)

A leader loves. A leader is humble. A leader serves no matter what their emotions are. Jesus established his position in our lives to prove that no title, accomplishment, or circumstance gives us an excuse not to serve others. As we continue, we will discover that Jesus has emotions just as we do. No, he didn't give his disciples a haircut, but he bathed their feet. He prepared them to serve others knowing it would help them through their grief after his death on the cross. **He gave them an example to follow.**

Read John 13:12–17. How did Jesus identify himself?

What is the significance of identifying himself in that way regarding the washing of feet?

What reason did he give according to verse 15?

| What is the result of doing the same? See verse 17.

| Can you identify a character trait in Jesus from this passage that is one we can learn from?

Dorcas served the widows in her community. They grieved when she died, but that is not the end of the story. Read Acts 9:36-42 to see what happened next.

As you read the widows' stories written in this book, you will see how serving others in their time of grief has helped them through it. I'm not sure we ever fully recover, but I do know from experience that serving others gives us a sense of fulfillment and purpose in our new beginning.

Jesus prepared disciples to serve without his physical presence. We are his disciples if we have faith in God through Christ Jesus and follow in his footsteps.

No longer do I call you servants,
for the servant does not know what his master is doing;
but I have called you friends,
for all that I have heard from my Father
I have made known to you.

John 15:15 (ESV)

And when the Lord saw her,
He had compassion on her
and said to her,
"Do not weep."

Luke 7:13 (ESV)

Chapter 3

River Stones

Lori Rohlinger

Only be strong and very courageous,
being careful to do according to all the law
that Moses my servant commanded you.

Joshua 1:7a (ESV)

I was wandering and felt lost.

It's amazing to look back at where I was when I first lost Greg. We spent four years of our lives fighting for his life and then the battle was over. Now I face a new battle. Who would I be without him? The worry and fear over my next steps and trying to figure out what was best for our children morphed into a severe identity crisis filled with doubt about who I was in Christ and the question of whether he still had a grand plan for my life.

I needed to figure out how to lead if I was going to be the best single mom and figure out what was next in life. I searched for strong leaders in the Bible—people who overcame struggles and obstacles but could still do incredible things for the Lord. I did a study on the life of Moses, and while he was not perfect, he was an amazing, powerful leader and motivator for God's children, Israel. I can't imagine spending half of my life in a palace, half of it as a nobody who tended sheep, then called to the greatest work the Lord had for me at eighty years old! But such is the life of Moses. All of his leadership and even his relationship with God was big and bold. My husband, like Moses, was larger than life. I wasn't.

The next leader Israel had, Joshua, in some ways, reminded me of myself. I felt a little sorry for him. Unlike Moses, he didn't speak face to face with God or perform miracles. Rescuing a nation from captivity or leading them through a forty-year desert journey wasn't something he did. Joshua might not be as flashy as Moses (although the falling walls of Jericho was pretty impressive), but he possesses a superpower that Moses didn't always have. Joshua was obedient to God.

To be a strong leader, I had a choice. Would I believe that God's loving touch shapes every part of my life, and he has an amazing purpose for me? Or was I going to listen to my worries and doubts, continue to wander and feel lost, thinking that God somehow failed me and my kids?

Daily, I remembered God's past help and blessings despite grief. I placed great value on reading God's Word and staying connected to him through prayer every day. Like Joshua, I learned blessings follow obedience.

I love Joshua chapter 3 when Joshua hears from the Lord on his next steps to lead the Israelites. "The Lord spoke to Joshua: 'Today I will begin to exalt you in the sight of all Israel, so they will know that I will be with you just as I was with Moses'" (Josh. 3:7 CSB). What an affirmation God gives to Joshua, reminding him HE plays just as important a role to God's divine plan as Moses. And God did the same in my life. While I thought my husband was the lead character and my job was to play the supporting role in life, I, too, have many abilities. God has given me so many opportunities to grow in writing and speaking and led me into more entrepreneurial pursuits that I would never try on my own! I am a walking billboard for the Lord that he will give you strength you never would have possessed without the trial of widowhood.

Though Joshua was not the leader like Moses, he was the leader Israel needed. Joshua obeyed God's instructions, and the Israelites crossed the Jordan River on dry ground. Don't let the impossible stop you from doing what God asks you to do.

Often, a way to remember the awesome things God did for the Israelites was to make a monument to memorialize what took place. Joshua told them to bring the river stones and stack them up on the land so that, "in the future, when your children ask their fathers, 'What is the meaning of these stones?' you should tell your children, 'Israel crossed the Jordan on dry ground'" (Josh. 4:21–22 CSB). So, they made a monument on the land, but in verse 9, we are told that Joshua also stacks twelve stones in the middle of the river as a reminder. Be aware that this was the flooding season. They wouldn't have seen the stones in the river until it was a dry season. That's when we need the reminder most. Yes, it can feel like we are drowning during the flood. It's when our lives feel dry and withered that we can let ourselves become bitter and angry, feeling like God has abandoned us and has no plan for our future.

If you doubt your forward momentum, remember the times God pulled you out of a dark place. Maybe you've never trusted him to help you out. Put your faith in him today. Pray and ask him to get you through your struggle today. Write it down. Afterward, describe giving it to God. He can make a way, even when there seems to be none. Remember, God sees you, God loves you, and if you will walk in obedience to him, he can't wait to bless you on your journey through widowhood!

Tips for Living Forward

Balancing new responsibilities can feel overwhelming, but take one day at a time. Prioritize tasks, seek support when needed, and trust God's provision to meet every need. Make a list of responsibilities your husband had with the family and ask God to help you make decisions for how to handle them.

Message of Hope – 3

Preparation for Belief

I am telling you this now,
before it takes place,
that when it does take place you may
believe that I am he.

John 13:19 (ESV)

It is a difficult thing to believe our loved one is gone when it happens, even more so when it is unexpected. Jesus wanted the disciples to accept his departure by telling them beforehand what would happen. Their faith was going to be tested, he would be betrayed, but they were to believe he was the Messiah sent from God to save the world.

Jesus was betrayed. He knew it was coming, and he knew who was the one to betray him. Read John 13:18–30.

> **According to verse 18, why were the things Jesus spoke of to take place?**

What reason did he give for the words he spoke? See verses 19–20.

Then he dropped an explosive statement in verse 21 that was so shocking, the disciples just looked at each other: "One of you will betray me." As he was saying this, what does it reveal about Jesus's emotion?

Another word for "trouble" is "sorrow." Jesus loved his friends, the disciples. He knew they would grieve his leaving. They were still not in a place of understanding why he would be betrayed. Betrayal hurts. There was a time when ministry volunteers betrayed us, and we did not understand. "Troubled" or "sorrowful" are mild words for the pain and rejection we experienced. But I am sure it was nothing compared to what Jesus must have felt knowing one in their midst would betray him.

> **Read John 13:28–30. How do we see from these vers-es that they did not understand why Jesus was saying these things?**

Just as God had a plan for why the betrayal of Jesus would take place, he has a plan for every tragedy we face. His plans are in advance, prepared beforehand for us to move forward in our belief and service. Jesus grieved just as we do. He relates to our sorrow. John 11:35 (ESV) tells us "Jesus wept."

Jesus performed miracles in life and death situations. When a widow's son died and Jesus saw him being taken out of the gate, he told her not to weep. Then a miracle occurred. He touched the bier and told the young man to arise. He had compassion for the widow, but the miracle was for the crowd of people gathered to belief. (See Luke 7:11-17).

We weep also when loss occurs and in our grief when others hurt us because they don't know what to say and don't understand because they have not been through it. Our feelings can betray us as we are buried in grief and feel hopeless. But Jesus has compassion for us and meets our emotional needs of the moment.

When he told the disciples of the betrayal with sorrow in his heart, **he was preparing them to keep believing in him** when all these things took place. Their faith must be strong when others wound with words and physical harm. This is what the Word of God does for us. It gives us hope to carry on when loss and grief threaten to consume us. This hope is our faith and belief in Jesus. The faith of our spouse took him to his heavenly home, and with our faith, we will one day see him again. Jesus went to prepare a place for us.

The blessing of him
Who was about to perish
came upon me,
And I caused
the widow's heart
to sing for joy.

Job 29:13 (ESV)

Chapter 4

Face-to-Face Impact

Kelly Kausen

I hope to come to you and talk face to face,
so that our joy may be complete.

2 John 1:12b (ESV)

Brendan called to update me on his end of our business, then added, "I wanted to bring this up earlier but did not feel you were ready yet. As you know, I am getting married in October in New York. I would like you to come, but no pressure. Can you think about it and let me know?"

I learned this is how God works with me when he wants me to do something. First, the idea is introduced. He lets me think about it to prepare myself, then pulls and sometimes pushes me forward. God does not always give me as much time as I had to think about doing this event, but this time, I needed every second. This was a big decision for me because I had gotten used to the small world created during the caregiving months, helping my husband fight for his life—and ushering my beloved home to heaven.

Brendan did not know my need for a warmup period on decisions, but the way he managed the suggestion was perfect for me. His first casual, verbal invitation came about six months after my wonderful husband, Scott, had passed. The way Brendan presented the invitation was balm for my soul.

Of course, I had heard about their plans for the wedding. It was to be outside on a seventh-floor terrace atop a building within

Rockefeller Square. It would start at dusk, so the lights and city would come alive and twinkle as the ceremony was ending. But could I go? Could I take part and not be a bother? I longed to be surrounded by laughter and joy.

First, I called Bruce and LaVonne, dear friends of my Scott and told them I wanted to go to the wedding, and asked if we could reschedule our golf date to celebrate Scott's birthday. LaVonne reported that something had come up with their schedule, too, so she encouraged me to go.

Somehow, this was going to happen. This had to happen. This is where I was supposed to be. Funny how God orchestrates the steps and prepares you for the next steps by having you practice smaller events. He does this before he shows you bigger plans, like a trip across the country in one weekend and back—all with a smile on my face, a pleasing disposition, and joyful countenance so that I might become a blessing to others.

Flying out on the morning of Scott's birthday was challenging because I had to leave my home by four in the morning. Arriving at the airport with plenty of time to spare, my stress and anxiety were low, because I was on schedule. I boarded the plane and sat next to the most wonderful person. His name is Elliot. I rarely talk to people on planes, but he was different. This young Jewish man from nearby Carlsbad was a blessing. We talked about several things: family, work, where he was going, and the occasions that were taking us across the country from San Diego to New Jersey and New York. He even provided me with suggestions about things I could do while in New York that would be easy to get to and fit into my schedule. It was like God had provided a personal travel agent!

The car service Brendan had suggested took me as planned from the airport. They texted me where to go outside and who to look for. A beautiful drive from New Jersey followed this smooth transition from plane to car and on to New York, with a flawless delivery to my hotel. As I was doing this, and taking pictures out the window, the driver, noting my actions, started pointing out things as we journeyed and soon, I noticed this was fun!

The next morning, I saw Brendan and met his aunts, Bonnie and Margaret, who I spent the day with touring sites and taking pictures. That evening, the temperature was perfect, the wedding glorious, full of love and happiness, and yes, magical! I realized that rooftop is where I needed to live at the moment. My Scott would have wanted me to enjoy myself, dance, laugh, and be present, and so I did.

I'm not sure they needed me to attend, but I am so glad they invited me. We need people around us to want us to be there. Let me share a nugget of wisdom that helped me capture God's heart about this need for people. Did you know the words in Greek for "face to face," in the opening verse, imply that our face is a weapon? Derived from the word *stoma* (stom'-a), meaning front or edge, or face or mouth, and from the prime root of *temno*, meaning to cut more decisively, comprehensive, not to use repeated blows, but a decisive cut. Regarding interactions, we understand that direct words spoken with all the cues that go along with our words carry more impact when shared "face to face." This Scripture gets even better when you see it is called an anarthrous construction, meaning it points to the quality of something. The quality of "face to face" confirms that presence is a present.

God in his sovereignty pre-planned for me to attend a wedding cross country, knowing the trip would help me realize my responsibility to get on with life. It is healthy for me to balance the treasured memories of the past with the hope of God's goodness in the future. Yes, the memories of my husband will come, and I am grateful for them as my heart and mind recall these precious moments. Yet, I now look forward to new moments and events that I know Scott would have loved, too. These things honor my husband, his joy, jokes, and his gift of always making people laugh.

Today is my responsibility and a gift. I am forever grateful for these people, family, friends, and fellow sojourners, and the opportunities they provide to fill my spirit with life, hope, and joy.

You have turned for me my mourning into dancing;
you have loosed my sackcloth and clothed me with gladness.

Psalm 30:11 (ESV)

Tips for Living Forward

Cherish the memories but let them inspire you to create new ones. Turn nostalgia into gratitude by journaling blessings from your marriage and sharing stories with loved ones to keep your husband's memory alive.

Message of Hope – 4

Preparation for Love

A new commandment I give to you, That you love one another:
Just as I have loved you, You also are to love one another.

John 13:34 (ESV)

God had a plan for the disciples, and he has a plan for us. He prepared them in multiple ways:

- He assured them of his love in John 13:1.
- He assures us of his love in John 3:16.
- He prepared them for service in John 13:5.
- He prepares us for service in John 13:15.
- He identified himself so they would believe in John 13:19.
- He taught us how to believe in John 13:30.

Why are these lessons important for a widow in grief?

Read John 13:31–35. It must have been devastating for the disciples when they learned Jesus would only be with them for a little while longer, but even more so when he said they could not go with him. He followed that information with instruction in the form of a command. It was not an option. What was it according to verse 34?

> What was your reaction when you learned your husband would only be with you a little while longer and you could not go with him? Did he give you any instructions for when he was gone?

As I visited the home of a family with children, the parents were leaving and gave one of the children instructions for staying with me, and he couldn't go with them. He was devastated to the point of running after the car, crying, "I want to go." My heart broke for him. When he went as far as he could, he came back to me and in a broken voice told me again, "I just wanted to go." All I could do was hug and love on him saying, "I know," until he quit crying.

For me as a widow, my cry was, "Don't go." But I know the loving arms of Jesus held me close through my broken heart until I could quit crying.

The Scripture doesn't tell us the disciples cried. It does tell us that Peter ran after Jesus saying he would die for him. But Jesus proved to him that he would be denied (see verses 36–38).

> Jesus gave them purpose, an action that put their focus on others in their loss. Can doing the same help you? According to verse 35, why did Jesus want them to love one another?

Jesus prepared the disciples to take on his mantle as ambassadors for Christ (see 2 Corinthians 5:20) so others would believe in him. Then in verse 36 we find his promise that even though they could not go with him, they would follow afterward.

This promise is our hope as well. We can be confident of going where Jesus is and where our loved ones are for those who believe. We cannot go with them now, but we will be with them later. Looking forward can help us through our times of sorrow. **He has prepared us for his love and to love one another.**

For the young child I was keeping, his parents told him he could not go with them then, but they would come back, and he would be with them again. What a beautiful picture this is of Jesus's promise to come again and that we would be with him forever.

Leave your fatherless children;
I will keep them alive;
And let your widows
trust in me.

Jeremiah 49:11 (ESV)

Chapter 5
Tragedy to Triumph
Sheryl Giesbrecht Turner

"For I know the plans I have for you," declares the Lord,
"plans to prosper you and not to harm you,
plans to give you hope and a future."
Jeremiah 29:11 (NIV)

"No!" I screamed as I fell to the floor. "There must be some mistake. It can't be true." But the doctors confirmed the truth: Paul was dead. I couldn't believe it. Paul had been so physically fit, in good health with no heart issues, but the motorcycle accident had produced multiple traumatic injuries, resulting in the heart attack that ushered him into heaven. Paul, my husband, pastor, and ministry partner was dead. My senses numbed as I tried to get a handle on reality; I struggled to process the newly presented facts. Going forward into a future without Paul did not make sense. The magnitude of this tragedy was too much to take in.

Through it all, I remembered the Scripture passage I had taught at the women's retreat not over eight hours earlier. The words gnawed on my raw emotions: "'For I know the plans I have for you,' declares the Lord, 'plans to prosper you and not to harm you, plans to give you hope and a future'" (Jer. 29:11 NIV).

My mind was fuzzy. Fear, uncertainty, and agony overcame me. Questions loomed. How could Paul's death "prosper" me? The Hebrew word for "prosperity" means "a good and hoped-for outcome." At that moment, I didn't get what I'd hoped for on earth, but could I expect God's hope? How could I sort through my doubts, fears, questions, and curiosities to continue to live a productive life? I felt smothered by distrust. I wanted so much to believe. In that dark moment, my own misgivings and skepticism hid the truth of God's hope. After the doctors told me that Paul was dead, I left the hospital with many doubts. But I learned to express them.

God, what is going on? I survived stage IV cancer; Paul and I fought it together, and now Paul is dead. Don't you love me, our family, our future?

Pastor Paul Giesbrecht's motorcycle accident was horrific, unexpected, tragic. It was my worst nightmare. That fateful day I began a blind trek down a lonely road through the valley of the shadow of death. It was the day I became a widow and a single parent, and my children were now fatherless. I learned not only about death but also about grieving and learned my crazy feelings of grief were normal. Grief is like an uninvited houseguest who won't go away. It is personal, and I discovered only I could grieve in my way. The most important thing I learned was how to be honest with myself. Although I didn't want to feel my losses, anguish, and pain, I discovered how to be in touch with my feelings and not deny them. The process was painful, just like the earlier emotional surgery with my counselor had been. It took time for me to heal, but once I understood my feelings, it helped if I communicated them to others who wanted to share my burden. Although I didn't know how I could find the way through that darkness and despair, God had proven himself to me in the past, and I knew I must trust his unfailing love, his constant faithfulness, and his strong presence.

I continued to renew my mind with the promise I'd questioned right after Paul's death: "'For I know the plans I have for you,' declares the Lord, 'plans to prosper you and not to harm you, plans to give you hope and a future'" (Jer. 29:11 NIV). I discovered additional Scriptures that encouraged my heart to trust God's timing for Paul's heavenly homegoing. "The righteous perish, and no one takes it to heart; the devout are taken away . . . to be spared from evil. Those who walk uprightly enter into peace; they find rest as they lie in death" (Isa. 57:1–2 NIV). My broken heart began to be put back together, one small piece at a time. "The Lord is close to the brokenhearted and saves those who are crushed in spirit" (Psa. 34:18 NIV). My faith began to grow. Instead of feeling overcome with sadness when I thought about Paul, my memories comforted me. Sometimes I laughed when I remembered a few of the crazy things we had done while dating.

I no longer began crying because of my loss when I recalled the happy times—the births of our children, wedding anniversaries, birthday parties, and family gatherings. Remembering these instances now helped my gloom to lift. When we choose to accept losses of any kind through choosing belief and push through them instead of turning over to doubt, growth takes place. What losses are you facing? Will you allow God to turn them into growth?

 **Tips for Living Forward**

With God's help, Sheryl learned to accept her loss. Look at a photo album if you have one to be reminded of joyful times. Thank God and allow him to transform your pain into a ministry of encouragement and hope.

Message of Hope – 5

Preparation to Know

From now on you do know him and have seen him.

John 14:7b (ESV)

As a child and young adult, I thought I knew Jesus. After all, I was taught to be a good girl from a good home and went to Sunday School. The church gave my age group Bibles with a picture of Jesus on the inside cover. Then in my late twenties I discovered that to know Jesus is to believe and receive him as personal Savior. This belief, confession, and receiving Jesus changed my life forever. Being good and going to church did not make me a Christian. Jesus did. Knowing him in a personal way has helped me survive the loss of my husband. And he will help you, too.

We continue the message of Jesus's preparation for the disciples in John 14. In chapter 13, we read about Jesus being troubled. Now we will read about his instruction to his followers not to allow their hearts to be troubled. Remember that another word for "trouble" is "sorrowful."

What are some things that trouble you?

According to John 14:1, what is Jesus's answer for how not to be troubled?

Read verses 1–7. Make a list from verses 2–4 of each statement of hope.

What was Jesus's answer to Thomas about knowing how to have this hope? See verses 5–7.

"I am the way, and the truth, and the life" (John 14:6 ESV). The scriptural meanings behind these words as found in the *Vine's Expository Dictionary*[2] and *Strong's Concordance*[3] are as follows:

- WAY – *The parting of a highway, crossroads* (see Isaiah 30:21). Metaphorically, *a course of conduct.*
- TRUTH – *The reality lying at the base of an appearance. Truth in all fullness and scope, as embodied in Jesus; he was the perfect expression of the truth. Sincerity and integrity of character.*
- LIFE – *Life as God has it, that which the Father has in himself and which he gave to the incarnate Son to have in himself (John 5:24, 26), and which the Son manifests to the world (1 John 1:2), and of this life men became partakers through faith in the Lord Jesus Christ (John 3:15). Jesus is the life of the believer.*

Simon Peter asked Jesus where he was going. Thomas asked how to know the way. And Phillip wanted him to show them the Father. What was Jesus's response to Phillip? See verses 9–11.

---

2   Vine, W. E. *Vine's Complete Expository Dictionary of Old and New Testament Words* (Nashville: Thomas Nelson Publishers, 1996).

3   Strong, James. *The New Strong's Expanded Exhaustive Concordance of the Bible* (Nashville: Thomas Nelson Publishers, 2010).

Do you sense a little frustration in his comments? It's almost like he is saying, "Are you kidding me! After all I've said and done, what don't you understand? Whoever has seen me has seen the Father."

The disciples thought they knew Jesus. But to know him is to know the Father. To know him is to believe he was sent by the Father, and he is God himself who came to earth in the form of man so all could know him by faith. God made every provision for the world to know him, and he came as Jesus to introduce eternity to us all.

Jesus came to prepare the world to know God in a personal way through him.

Now at this time while the disciples were increasing in number, a complaint arose on the part of the Hellenistic Jews against the native Hebrews, because their widows were being overlooked in the daily serving of food.

Acts 6:1 (NASB95)

Chapter 6

Legacy of Kindness

Karen Whiting

Do nothing from selfishness or empty conceit, but with humility consider one another as more important than yourselves; do not merely look out for your own personal interests, but also for the interests of others.

Philippians 2:3–4 (NASB)

My late husband, Jim, always thought of others, either saying words to brighten someone's day or through small acts of kindness, even picking roses off our trellis to bring to the office for the ladies. The children were young, and he never complained when he returned from work to a messy home. He'd hug me and say, "Looks like you had a tough day." Then he'd start picking things up, fold laundry, and get the kids to assist. His kindness filled our home and hearts.

His kindness, that mirrored my dad's kindness, attracted me to Jim when we first met. My father always said, "There's never too much kindness in the world." They both sprinkled it wherever they went. Instead of looking at problems negatively, he'd find something to laugh about.

He loved inviting people to dinner. Being practical, I felt dinner guests provided opportunities for the children to learn manners and practice hospitality, plus I enjoyed cooking. We teamed up with our talents and gifts.

Seeing my children follow their dad's example of kindness filled me with joy and pride. Like Jim, our children were outgoing. They thanked cashiers and complimented people on their clothing, eyes, or attributes. Our children always opened doors for people and smiled as they passed by.

After Jim passed, I realized he left behind his kind spirit with little surprises. I kept discovering the gifts he had prepared for me to find. Hidden in his shoes, I found my favorite chocolates. Hanging up with his clothes, I found a package that held some of my favorite hand creams and lotions. He even left gift certificates he earned online to be given for Christmas gifts to the grands. The first Christmas after Jim died, I looked for something in the glove compartment of my car and found a spare twenty-dollar bill. I'd been discovering quite a few bills Jim left in various places, but I had not seen this one before. I prayed and asked God to guide me to use it to bless someone—just as I knew Jim would have done. The next day at church, one member stood up and asked for prayer. He worked as a trash collector, and someone had gotten to all the stops before him and taken all his tips. He counted on the tips for presents for his family.

Jim always enjoyed chatting with this gentleman and I knew he would want him to have the twenty-dollar bill he had stashed in the glove compartment. It was only a little compared to his loss, but he told me it gave him such hope. He had appreciated Jim and felt Jim was reaching out from heaven to bless him and his family.

Passing on the money and my children's kindness awakened my heart to continue to reach out with kindness when possible. I realized I often overlooked noticing if someone looked sad or if a person needed a helping hand. As a busy mom with a huge list of things to do, I slowed down to look around more. Jim, six feet tall, could see more around him than I could see at one foot shorter. I continued the tradition we had of baking decorated Christmas breads for neighbors, even in the new neighborhood. As an author,

I encourage new writers and share titles of friend's books when they match something a person mentions. I may not cook as often, but when I bring a dish to a potluck, I often make one of Jim's favorites.

When others extend kindness, it makes me think of Jim and I thank God again for all the years he gave me with my husband. I'm not as quick with words as Jim, but I enjoy giving away little gifts. I send spiritual loving care packages that connect Scriptures with small, wrapped items. There's something comforting to rekindle the best qualities of our late spouse in our daily life and notice them in your family members. It's also heartwarming to recall the memories that made our loved one special. His photo makes me smile. I see kindness and laughter in his eyes.

As a widow, I suggest you list the qualities and activities you miss most. Then do those things to carry on the spirit that made your loved one so precious and unique. Consider what he complimented you on, what you enjoyed doing together, and what he did to make you smile. Continue those activities or do them differently. Enjoy favorite outings or restaurants with family or friends.

Tips for Living Forward

Karen honored her husband by continuing traditions that bring joy and meaning to life. You can do the same. Invite family or friends to join you in these traditions, making them a shared celebration of his legacy.

Message of Hope – 6

Preparation for Works

Truly, truly, I say to you,
whoever believes in me
will also do the works that I do…

John 14:12a (ESV)

Denial is a stage of grief. It questions the reality of what is to take place. Denial questions authorities such as doctors. When a patient is given unwanted news, he and his wife may go into a state of denying the truth they are hearing. This begins a long process of trying to understand and accept what will occur.

The disciples heard what Jesus told them about leaving. They had seen his miracles, but they were not at a place of accepting that he would really leave them. The same is true for us as women whose husbands have left us. We may not have been prepared for his leaving, but we can learn from these lessons Jesus gave the disciples for how to live once departure takes place. Denial delays acceptance. That is what the disciples were doing with their questions. They were not facing the reality of what Jesus was saying about leaving them.

> He assured them that the Father dwells in him and is who does the works he has done. Then he gave them their assignment. Read verse 12. Who will God work through when Jesus returns to the Father? How did he describe these works?

Jesus's works include his miracles, activities, and teachings to lead others to believe. God will do greater works through believers because of the Holy Spirit abiding within. These greater works cannot be accomplished in our own strength and ability, but only as God works through his Spirit in us.

It is because of his Spirit within us that we can overcome denial to accept the reality of our widowhood and do the works he places before us.

| Write the promise given in verses 13–14.

What great promises we have from Jesus. **We will know the works God has for us** as we pray and ask in the name of Jesus. We may be alone in our home, but God is not finished with us yet.

Bring justice to the fatherless
Plead the widow's cause

Isaiah 1:17c (ESV)

Chapter 7

A Changed Perspective

Susie Kinslow Adams

And now, God, do it again—
bring rains to our drought-stricken lives
So those who planted their crops in despair
will shout "Yes!" at the harvest,
So those who went off with heavy
hearts will come home laughing,
with armloads of blessing.

Psalm 126:6 (Message)

As I turned the calendar to August, I felt my spirit drop. Gone now three years was my best friend, my soul mate, my better half. Some have said, "It gets easier with time." Well, it doesn't feel that way today. The daily chores he took in stride continue to be mountains for me. I dislike asking for help. The world sees me radiating smiles and confidence; inside, I'm falling apart.

From the day we met, Russell was my rock—the one person in all my life I knew I could depend upon, rain or shine. He was my faithful support and guide as our marriage took me from a widowed house painter to a busy pastor's wife. He loved and supported me while encouraging my daily Bible studies and women's ministry endeavors. That anniversary date on the calendar still pulls my spirit down. The hole he left is big; my heart continues to break. As that fateful date drew closer, I could feel my spirit falling into a deeper sense of loneliness and despair.

I missed him.

I needed his hugs, his support, his encouragement.

I needed to see him snuggling in his cozy chair, waiting for his coffee.

Somewhere in the middle of my anxiety, hurt, and loneliness, my thoughts turned toward my mother. She lost parents, a husband, children, and so much more, yet remained strong and confident. God knew I needed her wisdom today. Mother would have told me in no uncertain terms that I needed to stop my pity party. "Carrol Sue," she would have said. "What do you think you are doing? If you keep dwelling on your loss, things will never be better for you. Why not think a minute about Russell—where he is and what he is doing instead of feeling sorry for yourself."

Knowing it was my thinking that had to change, I pleaded with God for forgiveness, as well as for peace and comfort. With my face washed and coffee in my hand, I headed for the back porch. With each breath of fresh air, my mind drifted to Russell and the heavenly bliss he must be experiencing. He spoke often of someday meeting the Bible characters he had studied and preached. I could picture him chatting with Abraham, Caleb, and old Moses.

My precious husband was in his thirties when he asked Jesus into his heart at a revival meeting. From that day, his gaze was toward heaven. And now he is home, healed, whole, and happy! He has no pain, no worries, no limits. I am sure the smile and twinkle in his eyes that warmed my heart here pales compared to his countenance with his Savior, Jesus Christ.

And, as if instructions fell from the sky, I knew I had to turn my self-centered pity party into a heavenly birthday celebration for him. A miracle took place in my heart that day. God changed my focus for this old temporary dwelling place to our permanent Home. Throughout the week, I shopped for his favorite candies: Milky Way, chocolate-covered peanuts, chewy mints, and more. At home, I added his favorite Scripture verses and sayings to dozens of snack bags filled with candies. Pity party be gone. I will celebrate this day in style.

Let the party begin.

We spent the entire day celebrating. When I had lunch at our favorite hangout, I took plenty of bags for the employees. A few surprised customers were also recipients of candies and well wishes. How fitting that August 21 was on Wednesday, a time for worship. Besides the candy bags, we needed gifts for a heavenly celebration. We created colorful book markers featuring a recent picture of the church and service times, finishing them with golden tassels. The icing on the cake for me was mid-afternoon as I handed candies out in the local bank, always being sure to mention the celebration was for Russell's third birthday in heaven. From her desk in the bank's lobby, Rachel took the candies with a smile and an unexpected reply. Looking toward heaven with a tear in her eye, she began singing to Russell in heaven, "Happy birthday to you, happy birthday to you, heavenly birthday dear Russell..."

Truth...

When I crawl into my bed each night, I would much prefer to pat his shoulder instead of his old pillow against my back. I have dozens of things to learn; I wish we would have talked more. But when the loneliness wearies me, I remember to look up and know "my redemption draws near" as well. My loving heavenly Father grants peace and grace for another day as I fall asleep in his arms.

Tips for Living Forward

Perspective is powerful. Choose gratitude each day, even in grief. Philippians 4:8 encourages us to dwell on what is true, noble, and praiseworthy. Find those moments, no matter how small, and let them lift your spirit.

Message of Hope – 7

Preparation for the Helper

And I will ask the Father,
And he will give you another Helper,
To be with you forever.

John 14:16 (ESV)

Up to this point in John chapters 13–14, Jesus has said many times that he is leaving. Now he continues to tell the disciples how he will be with them. How did he say this would happen?

He has taught them to know him and in verse 17, Jesus acknowledges that they do know him. Therefore, what is the promise made in verse 18?

The world won't see him when he leaves, but how will they see him? See verses 19–21.

> What does the one who loves Jesus do? See verses 23–24.

> According to verses 25–26, what will the Helper, the Holy Spirit, do?

As I think about the mission of Jesus and the help of the Holy Spirit, I am encouraged knowing what was true for the disciples is true for me, and also for you. These verses from 15–26 are filled with love and compassion from Jesus and for Jesus. Just as the Holy Spirit brings to mind all Jesus has spoken, the Holy Spirit brings to our minds the love and words of the one we lost, but who is now in heaven.

When I would tell my husband I loved him, he would always say, "I love you more." Recently while with my great grandchildren, I told the three-year-old that I love him. He looked me straight in the eyes with a smile and said, "I love you more." My heart melted at this golden nugget of love reminding me of the love of God and the love of my late husband. It is things like this that help us to realize the Holy Spirit is at work in our lives to meet our needs, and often he uses little children.

Jesus prepared the disciples for the Holy Spirit by his promise: "He will . . . bring to your remembrance all that I have said to you" (John 14:26b ESV).

When you gather the grapes
of your vineyard, you shall
not strip it afterward.
It shall be for the sojourner,
the fatherless, and the widow.

Deuteronomy 24:21 (ESV)

Chapter 8

A Shovelful of Grace

Sharon Engram

*And He has said to me, "My grace is sufficient for you,
for power is perfected in weakness." Most gladly,
therefore, I will rather boast about my weaknesses,
so that the power of Christ may dwell in me.*

2 Corinthians 12:9 (NASB)

I have always loved the number five. I've been told that it signifies grace, but this year, it is also the number of years since my precious husband left for his heavenly home. How can this be? So much has happened since my husband took his last breath on earth. We have experienced a worldwide lock down because of the COVID-19 pandemic. There have been government changes, higher cost of living, and wars across the globe. Through it all, God's grace, which is his provision, has been there for me every day. He's filled these five years with fun family time with my four adult children, fourteen grandchildren, and nine great-grandchildren. He's blessed me with new friends and even surprised me with a wonderful trip to Greece.

A couple of years into my new season of widowhood, I questioned myself, "Is it possible to move on? How do I cherish my memories yet also be open to new adventures?" I gave my life to serve the Lord as a young college girl, fell in love with a young minister and served alongside him for sixty years. How does someone move on from that? I cried out to the Lord to show me his plan for my future. God answered my prayer in a way I did not expect. During COVID-19, there was a writer's conference being offered on Facebook. I had always wanted to take a writing class, and I needed a distraction from loneliness, so I enrolled. Even though it was a stretch, the conference reminded me that God still has plans for me (see Philippians 1:6). During the virtual conference, I felt his nudge to write a book of short devotions to support widows. My daughter, who was also a pastor's wife and widowed three years before me, joined me in co-writing Surviving Widowhood, 40 Devotions of Hope, which was published in 2022. I never dreamed that at eighty, God would give me an opportunity to write a book to encourage widows. Our book has opened opportunities to speak to women's groups, retreats, churches, and podcasts. The Lord has given me a new ministry that I never imagined.

I listened to a story called "The Two Shovels" a few years ago. Someone asked a philanthropist how that worked. He responded, "I really don't know. I just shovel it out and God shovels it in, and he has a bigger shovel." On my desk, I have a small replica of the two "shovels." The large one represents God, and the small one represents me. Whenever I look at it, I am reminded that I can never out-give God. God has shoveled blessings into my life every day out of my pain and brokenness to bless and encourage women in their new season of widowhood.

The last five years have convinced me we can move forward as widows. It will be new and different from our married days, but I have learned that when I face loss, grief, and loneliness, I have three choices:

- I can let it define me.
- I can let it destroy me.
- Or I can allow it to give me strength.

I can't change my circumstances, but I can choose how to respond. The attitude to have is one I can choose for how I walk through the painful seasons of life. God has a bigger shovel, full of his strength, wisdom, grace, and peace. He heaps my small shovel full so I can pour out his love to others.

There is perhaps no one in Scripture who understood this more than the apostle Paul. In 2 Corinthians 12, Paul describes a thorn in his flesh, something he would have given away. God's word to Paul was, "My grace is sufficient for you, for my power is perfected in weakness" (2 Cor. 12:9 ESV). Grace is God's provision for each widow. He gives enough grace each day to feel His comfort, and it is sufficient.

Don't underestimate how God will use you. Pray with open hands and an open heart, asking for ways to move forward, to a new purpose, and be excited to live it. If you do this, he will open avenues for you that you never dreamed. His shovel is so much bigger. He will give you his power to trust him, his Word to guide you, and his abundant provision of grace to sustain you. May our response be, "Therefore I will boast all the more gladly of my weaknesses, so that the power of Christ may rest upon me. . . . For when I am weak, then I am strong" (2 Cor. 12:9–10 ESV).

What about you? Where are you on your journey forward in widowhood? Are you trusting God for your next step in life? Are you ready to ask God to pour his big shovel of strength, wisdom, grace, and peace into your smaller shovel so you can share his provision with others?

Tips for Living Forward

Try something outside your comfort zone; trust that God will provide the strength and wisdom you need. Step into new opportunities with courage and prayer (see Hebrews 12:1).

Message of Hope – 8

Preparation for Peace

Peace I leave with you;
My peace I give to you...
John 14:27a (ESV)

As we struggle with decisions about what is next in our lives, our minds may be in turmoil. I've always heard a new widow should not make any major decisions for at least a year following a death. I now understand why. My first year was filled with uncertainty and grief. I was in no condition to make any decisions. Oh, I tried, thinking I was okay. But I was not. I did not have peace with anything I was struggling to decide. Perhaps this describes you as well. I am so thankful for the Holy Spirit who led me through those months without making decision mistakes. He protected me from myself.

> **Read John 14:27–31. Jesus compared his peace with the world's peace. Think about our world today. What peace do you think the world gives?**

There is a movie about a female FBI agent entering a beauty contest to expose a threat of danger. I always laugh when I remember her walking on the stage, waving, and answering a question about what is important. She fake smiles and says, "World peace, of course."

"World peace" seems to be a term thrown around casually. It implies there is no violence of war, people, or nations. But when we read the words of Jesus, is world peace enough? Will a world at peace help us through our grief, loss, and decisions? According to the words of Jesus, it will not.

Jesus gives us peace by his Spirit. We can have it even when we cannot see him. We can ask for peace in the name of Jesus, and he will give it. It is a peace we can never understand; it just is.

When it is time to make decisions, how do you decide?

For me, I know it is a right decision if I sense the peace of God within my heart. If I am troubled, I will know it is not the right decision.

Jesus prepared the disciples to experience peace by the Holy Spirit. He does the same for you.

And the peace of God,
Which surpasses all understanding,
Will guard your hearts and your minds in Christ Jesus.

Philippians 4:7 (ESV)

The Lord protects the strangers;
He supports the fatherless
and the widow.

Psalm 146:9 (NASB95a)

Chapter 9

Strength from Within

Loretta Eidson

I can do all things through Christ who strengthens me.
Philippians 4:13 (NKJV)

I've quoted Philippians 4:13 throughout most of my life, but never had I understood the depth of its meaning until caregiving for my double-amputee husband before he departed this earth. Like a broken record, I repeated multiple times through my exhaustion, "I can do all things. He won't put any more on me than I can bear. I can do this."

My husband, Ken, literally needed me around the clock, and I could rarely sit down or sleep, thus the reason for my exasperated prayers. After months of constant attentiveness to his condition, I had no strength left. God, by his mercy and grace, miraculously sustained me and helped me fulfill my commitment to the man I loved. Otherwise, my body would have crumbled.

Then, early one Friday morning, my 24/7 caregiving responsibilities suddenly ended. I roamed the house aimlessly, stared out of the sunroom window where he'd been in hospice, and listened to the quiet. Doubts about how I cared for him bombarded my mind. Tears flowed. Had I done enough? Was there something else I could have done better? Did I always make him feel loved? Did I pray for him, encourage him, hold him? Why couldn't I remember? It was all a blur.

What do I do now? How soon was it too soon to empty his closet? No. I can't. But he wasn't coming back. What do I do with all the medicine, his wallet, his bank card, and all his tools? How am I supposed to care for the enormous flower garden he always manicured?

How do I go forward from here?

Again, I repeated that verse in Philippians: "I can do all things through Christ who strengthens me" (4:13 NIV). This time, a new meaning rose from the depths of my being. Christ still had a plan for me. He would grant me inner strength to face each new day and find the comfort I longed for if I'd surrender all my grief to him and let him guide me. I needed to seek God in reverence and adoration, rather than fatigue and desperation. It was time to lift my head and praise him for always being there and carrying me through the tough and sorrowful times.

Life without my husband would be different now, but I wouldn't be alone. God said he'd never leave me. I trusted his Word and allowed him to heal my broken heart. Ken was now in his new home with Jesus. A much better place than I could ever give him here on earth. He said goodbye, a bittersweet smile on his face, and urged me to find happiness. Now I needed to figure out what that happiness looked like.

I asked a friend from church, "When is it okay for me to smile and laugh again?"

"Whenever you feel like it. In your timing," she replied.

I pondered her answer, read my Bible, and prayed. Cried, too. Smiling seemed sacrilegious in the loss process. Oh, and laughter felt out of line. How was I supposed to respond to life without my husband?

Several months passed before I released the weight of grief and gave it to the Lord. It was a moment that freed me. Why had I waited so long? My blurry mental focus began clearing and realizing a new way of life emerged.

- It was okay to allow Ken to rest in peace.
- It was okay for me to laugh and remember the good times we shared.
- It was okay for me to take care of myself now.
- It was okay for me to move forward in life to live and love.
- It was okay.

Serving the Lord has always been my heart, even during those difficult times and the draining hours of caregiving. I learned valuable lessons through trials, and how I use that knowledge can, hopefully, help others.

- I realized that once a caregiver, always a caregiver, and as caregivers, we have gained experience with our keen eyesight and compassionate nature.
- We spot a need almost before anyone requests help.
- We are alert and sensitive to other's emotions.
- We embrace moments where we can encourage someone else.
- We have hands-on experience in being the hands and feet of Jesus.

So, I ask myself, what do I do now?

Life is too short to give up. There are hurting people all around that need to know that someone loves them. They need caring people to show kindness and acceptance. Therefore, I joined the mentoring program at my church so I can extend the love of Jesus with other ladies. I can point them to Christ, the one who is more than enough.

Besides mentoring and volunteering at my church, I returned to my computer keyboard to move forward on my novel-writing journey. Writing inspirational novels is another way I wanted to give back. It's a non-threatening means to express God's love to the world. Ken loved my novels and encouraged me to continue writing.

Coming to grips with loss is painful, but allowing ourselves to let it go releases all the mixed emotions attached to it. Yes, it's hard, but God's not finished with us yet.

God says we are overcomers, and with his help, I totally agree. There is life after loss. I encourage and challenge every widow to lift her head. Know that the Lord is good, and he cares about every detail of your life. Be strong and courageous. Move out from under the heaviness of grief that weighs you down and allow yourself to live in the freedom and splendor of Christ.

As the Bible says, "Weeping may endure for a night, but joy comes in the morning" (Psa. 30:5 KJV).

Tips for Living Forward

True strength comes from God (see 2 Corinthians 12:9). Loretta learned to be strong and productive. If you are able, step outside and breathe deep, or take a walk to gain physical strength.

Message of Hope – 9

Preparation for Obedience

Rise, let us go from here.

John 14:31c

The death Jesus would die on the cross would be excruciating. He knew it would be, but also that he would go to the Father where peace reigns. Following his promise of peace, he once again told the disciples not to be troubled or fearful. God would make something good out of the suffering of Jesus and his death that would benefit the world.

> **Are you beginning to see a repetition of Jesus's words to those who followed him? Write in your own words why you think repetition is important.**

> **Read verses 28–31. List what Jesus said he would do.**

> **What does he say about the Father?**

| What does he say about the ruler of the world?

| Doing as commanded is obedience. If Jesus does as the Father commands, what are the followers of him to do?

| According to verse 31, why does he obey the Father?

There are times when we experience hard things that we don't want to experience. There are times when we do things we don't want to do. But because of a bigger plan, we do them anyway. That was the situation of Jesus. Even though the ruler of the world had no claim on him, he knew he had to allow himself to be betrayed, captured, and crucified to fulfill the Father's purpose.

When our loved one is ill and ultimately dies, it is not something we want. We don't have a choice but to accept because we are not in control. But we can trust that our heavenly Father is in control and his love for us and our loved one will continue, endure, and support us in our loss.

Jesus repeatedly talked about love so the disciples would not walk away from faith and obedience to God. Obedience to the

Lord is not easy. Think about Peter when he denied Christ three times for his own protection. We cannot deny what God will do without damage to ourselves. When Peter realized what he had done, he wept bitterly. Clinging to God and his Word in our loss is what will guide us to whatever is next in our lives. When Jesus said to arise and go, it gave the implication of being led along. Jesus would lead; they would follow. They were leaving the place of safety and comfort from where they were, but they didn't know where they were going.

When I consider the minds of the disciples who were told over and again that Jesus would leave them, I can't help but wonder if they followed thinking, "What's next?" But they simply obeyed and followed.

It is a question we can ask God in our prayers. "Lord, I am following you. What is next for me now? Give me courage to get up and go where you lead. Amen."

Following in obedience where God leads is a good thing that reaps the benefits of peace. Jesus prepared the disciples for obedience.

But if a widow has children or grandchildren, let them first learn to show godliness to their own household and to make some return to their parents, for this is pleasing in the sight of God

1 Timothy 5:4 (ESV)

Chapter 10
God's Flight Instructions

Paulette Harris

Fear not, for I am with you;
be not dismayed, for I am your God;
I will strengthen you, I will help you,
I wll uphold you with my righteous right hand.

Isaiah 41:10 ESV

Jim and I were married almost fifty-five years, and we enjoyed a wonderful marriage, full of life, with unpredictable good times and not-so-good times. You know, normal most of the time. Although Jim was ill for many years, time seemed to move slower as symptoms showed up and he suffered. I believe we were both in denial. We hoped, prayed, and believed in God and his healing power.

The situation hit us one grueling day in Vanderbilt Hospital in Nashville, Tennessee, when his palliative care doctor hinted that there was no more to be done, and we should consider hospice care in the home. Exhausted, Jim pulled off the freeway on the way home and asked me to finish the almost three-hour drive. It was at that moment realization sank in for me and I held back tears as I let him fall asleep.

Transforming co-pilot to pilot began. This was a true sign because I never drove Jim anywhere. He told me lovingly it was his job to take me if we went somewhere together. I felt so bad; I couldn't even pray or cry that day.

As we prayed, things accelerated and a few months later he couldn't get out of bed without causing harm to himself by falling, so hospice put him into one of their beds with rails. He tried hard to get out by exercising his body in bed. By then, he still hoped he could beat this horrible disease—pulmonary fibrosis, caused by Agent Orange.

I felt like a child again. Our parents were gone and our sisters lived states away.

Thank goodness for hospice. I am so thankful.

The previous year, Jim ordered two little music boxes, one for my sister's birthday in November and one for me in August. Hers arrived the following spring, and we gave it to her then when they came for a last visit. Mine never came and we couldn't remember the name of the company, nor could we find a lost receipt.

The struggle became so difficult, and he suffered so badly; it sent me to my knees one night in the fall where I asked for help to let my precious man go where he could meet Jesus. No more pain and no more tears. I remember the moon was a huge harvest light. It was a color I'd never seen. The light seemed to be cast from the purest gold. Next to it was a large two-story building, casting the same color and light. I praised God for the comfort of this and went to share with Jim how much I understood about his pain and assured him I would be okay if he wanted to go home and what that home looked like. I tried not to cry in front of him, but I did, and he patted my hand. His favorite Bible verse was Isaiah 40:31, where we mount up on wings like eagles.

He fought hard, made it through the holidays, and ate Thanksgiving dinner, brave in his suffering.

Although it was difficult, that was his last meal. He decided he would make it to his next birthday, January 10, but he couldn't. Jim passed away on January 8. He was my pilot, best friend on earth, and a finer husband than I deserved. I am full of gratitude for the love and life we had together.

I went into NUMB mode, or what I call, autopilot. God took the seat of Pilot. That lasted a whole year. God did everything and sent everybody I needed to do the tough job of settling things and starting a new life.

When I prayed, I asked God several times, what was I supposed to do now? What was my purpose for the rest of my stay here on earth? I felt lost. I depended on Jim or my parents to help make my decisions, especially when I wasn't confident in which way to go. My work was writing for God's people, sharing his love, hope, and faith with readers. But, to many, it was my hobby, keeping busy in quiet times of reflection. Should I now be doing something else? I found I loved to write screenplays a few years prior, and it was a fun outlet for me to write. I studied the craft hard and dug in during COVID-19 with extra online classes.

The day Jim went to be with Jesus, everyone, including hospice, family, and friends, left and there was no one in the house. The doorbell rang and after realizing I was alone, I went to answer and there was no one there. But there was a small box on the front step. I picked it up, puzzled because there were no labels or a hint of where it came from or what it was. I opened it and, to my surprise, it was my little music box. It was an old-fashioned reel-to-reel projector, and it played a beautiful song. This sign seemed to be from Jesus and Jim that I needed to continue to write.

A month after this, I got a call from an old acquaintance that I hadn't kept in touch with for several years. He and several old writer friends invited me to a special writer's retreat. I argued, feeling unworthy, not good enough, sometimes too raw and emotional. And with no confidence, I felt like a mess. However, God knew this was part of healing my broken heart. They knew it, too, and I realized this was part of my purpose: to continue to write with faith, hope, and love to share God's Word of encouragement in a hurting world. God and Jim wanted me to attend and I'm thankful to those who didn't give up on me when I was so ready to give up on myself.

Now I'm God's co-pilot. Often when I feel afraid, the plane tries to go into a spin out of control or the wings tip up and down and the engine sputters. God reminds me he sits in the pilot seat next to me. There are big angels under each wing. They steady the plane and hold it up. He jumps the engine for me. God assures me that Jim is okay and that I still have work to do. My Pilot will call me when I'm finished with my purpose.

I have to be honest here. I still have good and bad days when I'm alone or people don't understand, and they are busy with their own lives and families. Sometimes I feel left out but, thank goodness, I have a wonderful Stephen Ministries mentor, and she is so helpful. I recommend this to whoever might feel lonely after losing a spouse. You are never alone; God always provides. The first year was autopilot. God has given me a new flight plan, and now I find myself in all kinds of weird circumstances. I'm glad God is the Pilot. He checks the plan and makes new decisions, corrections, and changes of direction. "Help, Jesus!" I cry.

What have I learned? Trust has been a big issue for me, but God is faithful, and I've let him choose others in my life to help me. I pray and try hard to "listen" to that still, small voice that cautions me.

I'm praying for each person who reads this and hope my journey somewhat encourages them. If I can make it, you can as well. God didn't promise us a rose garden, but what he did promise is that there is a special way for each of us to walk. You don't need to be fearless—just willing to take the initial steps. He understands and so do these authors, as we love you back into life without your loved one. God is long-suffering and understanding and wants the best for us. For me, it is the assurance that he sees and knows all. He's our great healer.

Thank you, dear Father. May you bless and heal each reader as they soar on wings of eagles and continue their flight home with you by their side. Use them for your glory, precious Jesus, as we give you the control over our lives. We praise you in the lovely name of your Son, Jesus Christ.

Tips for Living Forward

As women alone, we now make our own decisions without the valuable input from our husband. But our decisions should be made by seeking counsel from God and his Word. As we trust him with our future, he speaks through his Word and prayer to guide our decision-making process.

Message of Hope – 10

Preparation to Abide

If you abide in me,
and my words abide in you,
ask whatever you wish,
and it will be done for you.

John 15:7 (ESV)

Ask whatever you wish. We have seen those words before. Again, we find repetition in Jesus's teaching. When he repeated something it was to emphasize and affirm a point. It was to make it clear that what he was saying was important to remember.

Standing at the bedside of a woman close to death, I began to sing "Jesus Loves Me" and "Amazing Grace." Even though this woman's eyes were closed, and she was not speaking, she mouthed the words as I sang. How could she do that? Repetition throughout her life of singing those songs in church. They were meaningful to her, and she did not forget, even in her physical condition.

"Jesus loves me, this I know. For the Bible tells me so."

Can we even count the number of times Jesus talked about love in these chapters of John? He wants us all to remember that no matter what happens in life, "Jesus loves me, this I know." How? Because we have studied the Bible, seen his words, and followed where he leads. There is such comfort in that.

> **Read John 15:1–17. In these verses, Jesus now tells the disciples what is expected of them. They are to abide in him when he is gone. How can they do that? Look back to how he can live within us and write your observation. See John 14:26 and 14:4.**

To abide is to continue in faith, hope, and love as we dwell with Christ. Jesus used the example of a vine and branches to explain how to abide by his Spirit. We know if a branch is to survive, it must stay connected to the vine. If it breaks off, it dries up and is useless.

How did Jesus identify himself and the Father?

What do you think is the meaning of verse 6 when it says the branch that does not abide is thrown away and withers?

There are some who would take advantage of widows saying they are not Christians when they don't abide in Christ. We must know the difference between what is true and what is false. When presented with new relationships and opportunities, we must examine the lives of those involved. Do their actions and words reflect one who abides in Christ? Is there consistency in what they say with how they live? We need to do our research and check the facts before entering any new relationship or opportunity. Ask God for wisdom and for anything ungodly about the situation to be revealed for your protection.

> **Read verse 5. What do we see in the one who abides in Christ?**

> **What is the result of being apart from Christ? See verses 5–6.**

> **Verse 7 repeats something about prayer that Jesus said before. Here he repeats it in a different way. What are the two conditions given for answered prayer?**

This, then, is the answer for us at all times, but especially when presented with new relationships or opportunities: prayer, Jesus, and God's Word. **Jesus prepared the disciples to abide in him.**

and then as a widow until she
was eighty-four.
She did not depart
from the temple,
worshiping with fasting and
prayer night and day.

Luke 2:37 (ESV)

Chapter 11

Precious Moments

Kaye Johns

Pray without ceasing.

1 Th 5:17 (ESV)

The pain of my grief was sharp and overwhelming. But from the first moment, I was at peace and resting in the Lord, though I cannot remember anything else about the two months following Jim's service. When Jim died, I was emotionally numb. I went through the memorial service and the days following, holding myself together when others were present, grieving when alone.

For about two months, I dropped out of everything, including church and my ministry work. Returning to church was the most difficult step I had to make, though we were members of a loving and caring class. I think I didn't want to face the "How are you doing?" questions.

What brought me through these early weeks and continues to sustain me is, of course, my deep and abiding relationship with the Lord. My first morning without Jim, I put on worship music and filled my heart and prayers with worship. Worship lifts my spirit and always fills me with joy.

Moving forward was a day at a time. I simply picked up the reins of responsibility again. I'm blessed with children and grand-children who love me and are attentive, and I've made it a point to be involved in all family activities. Those relationships are priceless and healing. Jim's picture is on the face of my phone. It is always visible and goes everywhere with me. I continue to thank God for the fifty years he allowed us.

The Lord has sustained me, as he will anyone who has a close, personal relationship with him. He is faithful. My encouragement to others who have lost loved ones is to run into the Lord's arms. My prayer for them is that they will allow themselves the freedom to experience their own personal season of grief. We all grieve differently, and we mustn't let anyone make us feel we have grieved too little or for too long, or that we have or haven't been engaged with others as they think we should.

We must let grief have its way. My prayer is that they will come through their unique season of grief in a healthy way, and never lose the joy of precious memories.

Tips for Living Forward

Kaye learned to get out of isolation and seek others. If you're spending all your time at home grieving, encourage yourself to go outside, take a drive, or visit a friend. Be ready to respond when God moves in your life. Stay attuned to his voice through prayer and Scripture. Step forward in faith, knowing he is leading you to a new beginning.

Message of Hope – 11

Preparation to Bear Fruit

By this my Father is glorified,
that you bear much fruit
and so prove to be my disciples.

John 15:8 (ESV)

This passage of Scripture on fruit bearing is so perfect in describing a good friend of mine. She and her husband began a prayer ministry in their home so many years ago, I can't even count. There were five couples that participated each Friday evening. All five of those couples later entered ministry. We were one of those couples.

The host couple's prayer ministry grew to the extent they were being asked to hold prayer conferences all over the nation, and even overseas at one time. They were bearing fruit everywhere they went. Today, both our husbands are with Jesus, but my friend continues the prayer ministry. You now know her too from reading her story in chapter eleven. Kaye Johns has been a good friend and spiritual mentor of mine since I was in my thirties. I love her dearly and can honestly say I am one of her fruits.

Jesus used the illustration of himself as the vine and believers as the branches that are connected to the vine. Just as the grapevine is nurtured by the vinedresser, the vine nourishes the branches as its roots soak up water and nutrients from the soil. When we think of this process, we see the word "abide" as a picture of believers being nourished by the life of Jesus and nurtured by the love of God. The result for the vine branches is fruit. The result for the believer is making a difference in the lives of others for God's glory. That is our fruit.

To be sure we understand, according to verse 8, how do we prove to be disciples of Christ? What glorifies God?

According to verse 9, what do we abide in?

What is the result we see in verse 11?

Jesus feeds us by his Word. We are nurtured and nourished by his love and comfort. As we live in him, we grow spiritually and should be bearing fruit. The fruit is an image of good results coming from the life of a believer which brings benefits to others through the gospel of Christ.

Once again, we see a repeated phrase in verse 12. What is it?

How do we become friends with Jesus? See verse 14.

Jesus concluded this portion of his message with a summary of verses 1–15. We as believers are chosen with a mission to do what? See verse 16.

The message of loving one another affirms in our hearts and minds the importance of the statement. This is what helps us to move beyond pain and grief. God's everlasting love poured out in us and through us gives us purpose for not isolating ourselves after loss. There are three essentials for life: faith, hope, and love. The greatest of these is love—**the love of God for us and through us as we abide in Christ and bear fruit for his kingdom.**

And there was a widow
in that city who kept coming
to him And saying, 'Give me
justice against my adversary'.
'...yet because this widow keeps
bothering me, I will give her justice, so that she will not beat me
down with her continual
coming.'

Luke 18:3, 5 (ESV)

Chapter 12

Wait and Wonder

Louise Tucker Jones

Be strong and courageous. Do not be afraid; do not be discouraged, for the Lord your God will be with you wherever you go.

Joshua 1:9 (NIV)

I needed a ride. He needed money for gas. That's how we met. Not quite eighteen years old, I was already engaged to my high school sweetheart, who picked me up at college for weekend trips home. But not that week. So, a friend got me a ride with someone I'd never met.

No problem. It was only a ride. At least that's what I thought until I met the tall, blue-eyed, dark-haired driver with a teasing personality and a little egotistical attitude. Therefore, my engagement didn't last. Though it took a few more rides for us to get to know each other well, I can honestly say it was love at first sight. Carl Jones stole my heart that very moment and for a lifetime.

Married for forty-five years before Carl's journey to heaven, we saw the best and worst of life and losing Carl was definitely one of the hardest. What do you do when the person you loved and depended on most is suddenly gone? Most Christians would tell you to turn to God. And yes, I did, but I did so in anger. Oh, you can't get angry with God, people would say. Well, yes, you can, and I did, and so do a lot of other wives who become widows.

Why would God allow this to happen? We had already lost our middle son at three months old, and our daughter died just thirty days before Carl. Our youngest son, Jay, had Down syndrome and inoperable heart disease. He lived at home. The world felt empty without his father, and my eldest son's distance made the ache in our hearts unbearable.

Not only did I have a broken heart, but so many responsibilities that Carl always handled—the house, vehicles, acre yard, but most of all, Carl's help at home with Jay. He was the best of dads. Both of our sons missed him, and I felt abandoned. Why wouldn't I be angry? I questioned God. Yelled at him. Cried a million tears. But God never turned his back on me. I always knew he was with me. Even in my anger, I knew he was beside me, loving me in my pain.

I had no grand plan about how to move forward, but I was a columnist for a local magazine, so I let the world know how much I missed my husband. This brought an avalanche of emails from other widows, just wanting to talk to someone who knew how they felt. I would respond to their messages and soon I had several ladies following me, so I decided we should meet. I had no thoughts about leading a support group. I was meeting with like-minded friends. But just in case there were other ladies who might want to join us, I wrote in my column about a designated place and time that some widows would be meeting and welcomed anyone who wanted to join us.

I expected a dozen ladies, so we set up twenty chairs, then we set up more and more chairs. Women streamed into the room of all ages and stages of widowhood, each telling their story to someone who would listen. Interesting that God brought a widow for every year I was married, forty-five women, for forty-five years. We met once a month, and guess who the designated leader was.

Sometimes we met just to talk and share, but I also arranged speakers for meetings—bereavement counselors, estate planners, yoga instructors, even police officers teaching safety for widows. In one meeting, we had a fun jewelry party, and we often had dinner together at a restaurant. There was laughter, tears, and lots of love. I realized this was from God and we needed to honor him by opening each meeting with a prayer.

I never planned to lead a widow support group. I just did what God placed before me. I believe that's how he helps us move forward. He uses our talents, our gifts, our friends, our families, and our own unique personalities. I was a writer and there was an audience who needed my words. God used what was right in front of me, allowing others into my pain and even my joy.

It has been thirteen years since my husband relocated to heaven and I still miss him every day, but not with the pain I had soon after his death. My son, Jay, and I spent eleven years with just the two of us at home. We became a unique family. Though I always miss Carl, I'm always looking forward.

And now my sweet Jay, who loved to sing and dance to praise music, is also in heaven with his dad and Jesus. So, I'm learning to navigate grief all over again, just like I did with Carl. I pray. I listen. I sing and read Scripture. I write. I tell stories about Jay, and I often cry. It's another very hard journey, so I "wait and wonder" where God will take me. And I think that's the key to getting through grief. Being open to the waiting, knowing there will be struggles but also surprises. There will be hardships but also beautiful memories.

I claim God's love daily, giving all those hard places to him, knowing he has a plan. I may not know what that plan will be or how it will work out, and without my husband, that can sometimes be scary because I want his input. But God's Word tells me not to be afraid, so I pray for his guidance and wisdom. I pray for faith to take each new step, knowing God loves me and wants the best for me. And knowing it's okay to "wait and wonder" in my grief, but also knowing God will be with me wherever I go and whatever I do.

Tips for Living Forward

Waiting can feel like time wasted, but God works in the waiting. Louise learned to meet with others who had experienced loss. What can you learn from her story to help you look to the future?

There are times of indecision and confusion, when even the most willing person, who eagerly desires to serve the Lord, does not know what direction to take. So, what should you do when you find yourself in this situation? Should you allow yourself to be overcome with despair? Should you turn back in cowardice or in fear or rush ahead in ignorance? No, you should simple wait—but wait in prayer.

– Mercy A. Gladwin from *Streams in the Desert*[4]

---

4   Mercy A. Gladwin quote. L. B. Cowman, *Streams in the Desert* (Nashville: Zondervan, 2006).

Message of Hope – 12

Preparation for Sorrow

Truly, truly, I say to you,
you will weep and lament,
but the world will rejoice.
you will be sorrowful,
but your sorrow will turn into joy.

John 16:20 (ESV)

Jesus tells of his resurrection and that he would come to the disciples again. Through the gift of his Spirit, he would remain with them forever. But as his followers, they would suffer. His purpose in coming to them after his resurrection was to impart life to them.

> Read John 16:16–24. How would the disciples respond to the departure of Jesus? See verse 20.

Jesus predicted tears and sorrow. Then he used the example of a woman in labor pains during childbirth to make a point. What point is he making according to verse 21?

List the promises made in verse 22.

What makes joy full? See verse 24.

There is a great lesson for us in these verses. As women, some of us know what childbirth is like. And we also know what happens inside us the first time we hold and look at a precious newborn baby. Sorrow and pain take a backseat to the love and joy we experience.

These verses have shown us that pain and sorrow are for only a short time, but the fullness of joy in Jesus cannot be taken away from us.

Sometimes, the pain of loss is like a darkness trying to settle in and stay. We cannot see anything good coming out of our experience. We are not joyful. But if we are faithful to move forward and not give up, the mercies of God will guide us through. We may never experience the joy we had with our spouse, but joy with Jesus cannot be taken away from us. It is a different kind of joy that continues within us even in our darkest days. God works mysteriously in us, and we need not be afraid of what is next. Somehow he will bring goodness and productivity from all our pain and tears as we faithfully love and follow him.

From my own experience, I think the way this works is that when we are serving others, we have a sense of fulfillment during that time that brings joy. Then when we are home alone and the grief returns, we can know there is still joy to be found.

Think about something that brings you joy and take action to bring whatever it is to life in you once again.

Jesus prepared the disciples for the sorrow of his departure by setting their focus on what comes after the sorrow—joy.

If any believing woman has
relatives who are widows,
Let her care for them. Let the
church not be burdened,
So that it may care for those
who are truly widows.
(without family).

1 Timothy 6:16 (ESV)

Chapter 13

First Time Single

Virgie Mae Finn

*He who dwells in the shelter of the Most High
will abide in the shadow of the Almighty.*

Psalm 91:1 (ESV)

At fifteen years of age, I met Thomas, who was sixteen. We started double dating with my sister and her boyfriend. Tom and I became engaged when we were eighteen and nineteen and married a year later. Together, we had three children. This family has grown to nine grandchildren and eight great-grandchildren with twins on the way. I went straight from my father's house and authority to my husband's house and authority. When Tom died at seventy-five, I became single for the very first time!

Tom's health started deteriorating six months before his death. I was his primary caregiver, although I had physical support from my younger son. After a brief hospital stay, the doctor called the family in and, at Tom's request, moved him to hospice care because his pain and organ failures were so extreme. The family could receive hugs and last words of advice, wisdom, and sometimes unintended humor, as per medication. After one night in hospice, he passed the next morning, leaving me a widow. In this new state of singleness, my mind and heart were numb for a while. I walked from his room at the Hospice House through their library and a picture on a shelf caught my eye. Painted on it were the words from Psalm 91:4 about God protecting me and covering me with his wings. I claimed it as a personal message from God.

After the mental numbness had cleared, a couple of months later in Bible study, a classmate recommended a Christian financial advisor who was not only qualified in finances but also encouraging and helpful in so many other areas of need and in completing insurance forms. So many Scriptures emphasize GOD's concern for widows and orphans. I claimed God's promises, and he has sent me a qualified helper every time I needed someone and at just the right time!

I had seen widows who were bitter and angry with GOD for robbing them of their everything, even after years had passed. I had already decided that I would not choose that path. Instead, with the freedom I had as a widow, I could be and do anything and go anywhere I felt GOD leading. I wanted to make GOD smile when he thought of me. I looked at my new season in life, just as I had done as a new wife and mother, with joy, enthusiasm, and a sense of adventure. I pondered, what is GOD going to do through me, or better yet, what am I going to allow GOD to do through me?

Everyone needs a purpose—a reason to get out of bed in the morning and start a new day. You need to know someone, or something, is counting on you. Being a caregiver may be taxing on your whole being, but out of love, duty, and responsibility, we continue. But when it ends, after grieving and resting, we need to find GOD's purpose for our life. Being obedient to him is a full-time job.

One decision I made was to learn American Sign Language to keep my mind alert and growing. As I had no one to practice with, I got up the courage to sing and sign with songs on Sunday mornings in my pew at church. I was anxious every time I prayed or spoke in front of people, but in time, I overcame my anxiety about signing by realizing and believing that whatever I do for the LORD, I do for an audience of one! I had to think about the meaning of a word or phrase to find the proper sign to use. Singing and signing enhanced my personal worship. I gained confidence through other worshipers sharing how much they appreciated my signing. I am self-taught from an ASL book and online help. I use it now to do my part with our senior ministries for senior living facility residents. I received encouragement from our missions pastor, who returned from a trip to Senegal, West Africa, after having learned of a new school for the deaf that is now a part of our Bethlehem Christian Academy. He encouraged me by signing me up for the next Senegal mission trip! Less than a year after Tom died, at age seventy-five, I joined our mission trip to Zambia, helping in Vacation Bible School at their BCA. Going to Senegal would be my second time in Africa, something I could do as a widow. Because of a stroke in 2023, I canceled any return trips. It was a difficult but necessary decision to make after becoming too helpless to travel. I am still working on strength and balance to be what they once were, but in the meantime, there are local ministries in which I can get involved.

I have become a prayer warrior—something I can do even with physical limitations. I pray for guidance, strength, and discernment and work at staying connected to people, whether it is strangers who check out my purchases, church members, neighbors, or friends. They became family to me. Some have even adopted me for family celebrations and get-togethers. But that would not last long or repeat itself if I gave myself over to negative conversation. I have learned no one wants to keep company with a constant complainer, so I keep an attitude of gratitude, play uplifting music, listen to the Bible on my phone, check on others, and I am even learning to play more musical instruments. I have learned you are never too old—or too alone—to learn, love, help, and obey GOD's call in your life. I feel blessed because God has called me, and I have followed.

Deuteronomy 33:25 (NKJV) says, "As your days, so shall your strength be."

Isaiah 46:4 (NKJV) says, "Even to your old age, I am He, and even to gray hairs I will carry you!"

Tips for Living Forward

Virgie learned sign language as a practical way to help others. Learning a new skill or hobby can be a form of healing. Ask God to show you ways to grow. Embrace the process as an opportunity to rediscover joy and creativity.

Message of Hope – 13

Preparation for Truth

But when the Helper comes,
whom I will send to you from the Father,
the Spirit of truth,
who proceeds from the Father,
he will bear witness about me.

John 15:26 (ESV)

According to John 15:26 and 16:12–13, how is truth revealed?

Why did the disciples have to wait for the Spirit of truth to be led into all truth? Why didn't Jesus do it then? See verse 12.

> **From whose authority would the Spirit of truth speak? Read Isaiah 41:9 for insight.**

> **Look up the definition of the word "declare." Write how this applies to what the Holy Spirit will do.**

God speaks through the Holy Spirit to reveal what people of God need to know in the moment. But just as Jesus had much to say but didn't because the disciples couldn't bear it, neither can we. We have many questions for God about the timing of death, but we will not know in advance because we cannot handle all God knows and does. We will never understand the answer to why. *Lord, why did he get sick? Lord, why did you take him now? Lord, why did he have to suffer?* The answer is, God knows, and we do not. Perhaps because we couldn't bear to know.

However, we can know truth by the Spirit of God.

The truth we have a difficult time accepting is that of being a widow. However, that is not our identity. As believers, we are women of God. Therefore, greater truth is the love of God through Christ Jesus who sent his Spirit to help us through this time in our lives.

Jesus prepared the disciples with the promise of sending the Spirit of truth to reveal the truth of God.

She who is truly a widow,
left all alone, has set her hope
on God and continues in sup-
plications and prayers
Night and day.

1 Timothy 5:5 (ESV)

Chapter 14

Love Never Ends

Katherine Pasour

The Lord is gracious and compassionate,
Slow to anger and rich in love.

Psalm 145:8 (NIV)

"Love you, babe."
From the peaceful interlude between sleep and awake, I heard his voice. I reached to touch him and whispered, "I love you, too."

But his side of the bed was empty.

Alertness set in like storm-driven ocean waves crashing into shore. I sat up and my eyes confirmed what my mind already knew. He wasn't there. My husband had died several weeks earlier, after a heroic battle against cancer. The vacancy beside me on our bed mocked me, a stark and silent reminder of my loneliness.

Whose voice had spoken? Was it Bob's voice, one I longed to hear again to say those words we shared each night? I hadn't had a dream, at least not a visual one. Yes, Bob spoke to me.

Loss and Anger

Illness brought down my hard-working man. We were in the middle of the pandemic, isolated during his illness and following his death. Left behind, I occupied myself by working in the yard and completing numerous projects my husband had put off over the years. My emotions ranged the spectrum between anguish, sorrow, and anger. Physical labor became my best stress reliever. The sense of accomplishment I felt in completing needed work on the house and farm brought some satisfaction.

God had been with us during Bob's illness, and he especially granted me the strength and endurance to care for my husband. But afterward I didn't hear my heavenly Father's voice. Perhaps it was because of my anger—at God for not granting healing—and at Bob for dying with so much left undone. I poured out my pain to our Father; I cried out my loneliness and despair, and I shouted my frustrations to an empty house.

> *My dear brothers and sisters, take note of this:*
> *Everyone should be quick to listen,*
> *slow to speak and slow to become angry,*
> *because human anger does not produce*
> *the righteousness that God desires.*
>
> James 1:19–20 (NIV)

I knew my anger at God was wrong, but anger seemed easier to bear than the agony of sorrow and grief. Where was my "best" now? In response to my grief and anger, I made myself as busy as possible—on the farm, in the house, and back to writing my blog, articles, and books. I coped by pushing myself to exhaustion and avoiding dealing with my despair.

When it came time to reopen the church after COVID-19, I resisted returning. We'd always gone together, and this was another reminder that Bob was gone. I forced myself to enter the building, but his empty place in the sound room, the kitchen, on the roof making repairs, or anywhere I looked, proclaimed his absence.

Bob wasn't there.

He was in the cemetery behind the church.

Where Was God?

God was everywhere, but I struggled to find a moment in my "do more" attitude to listen to him. I ranted at him, but he didn't leave me. I distanced myself from my Father in my anger and grief, but he patiently waited. God was gracious and compassionate toward me. He showed his love and convicted me of my anger. Our Father doesn't hold grudges, but covers us with his love, bringing peace and comfort to a broken heart.

LORD my God, I called to you for help, and you healed me.

Psalm 30:2 (NIV)

My healing came in slow increments. As I engaged in church activities again, I noticed my attitude changed. No longer was my primary motive to be the very best to achieve goals I set for myself.

My goal became to serve—to see a need and take care of it. But this time, I didn't feel obligated to do it all myself. I worked with others, gathering a group to work together.

With the Lord as my guide, being a servant brought light to my darkness and filled the emptiness with love instead of anger.

Through God's gifts of love and mercy to me, I could forgive my Bob for leaving me—and for the tasks he'd left undone.

The Journey of Grief

The journey of grief doesn't end. Instead, grief is an ongoing road, paved with challenging hills (the trials we face) and dark valleys (the deep sorrow). Grief is like a roller coaster ride—we climb the steep incline and find brief glimpses of joy, then we plunge downward into depression and despair.

But there are those along the path who pray for us and befriend us (if we let them). Service opportunities appear and these tasks we do for others ease our burdens.

Most importantly, God is with us each step of the journey. He is ready and willing to take us in his arms when we need him most. He sends loving friends and family to surround us. And he presents opportunities to serve others.

We will always miss our loved one. They will forever be in our heart, our mind, and our memories. Even though he hasn't spoken to me directly, his actions have left a lasting legacy of joy and fulfillment. The memory of his message to me amid my deepest sorrow reminds me our love forever remains a part of the two of us.

The love we share with our spouse doesn't end when they leave us to be with Jesus. Love is always there in our hearts and in our memories.

Love never ends.

Tips for Living Forward

Anger is a natural part of grief. Katherine reached a point of recognizing how it was hindering her from moving forward. Ask God to help you process anger and grief in healthy ways. Find outlets like journaling, talking with a Christian counselor, or serving others. Clean out the closet and donate his clothing when you are ready.

Message of Hope – 14

Preparation for Tribulation

In the world you will have tribulation.
But take heart; I have overcome the world.

John 16:33b (ESV)

The time is near to departure. Jesus knows it. The tribulation he spoke of in this chapter refers to the hard times to come and the suffering the disciples will experience on earth. He speaks plainly to the disciples, and they finally get it.

> **Which verse shows us the disciples finally believed everything Jesus said?**

> **Once they made this confession of belief, Jesus breaks the news that all will not be easy for them. According to verse 33, what word describes what they will experience?**

| **What reason did Jesus give for why they should "take heart"?**

Everything about Jesus gives hope for the disciples then, and for generations to follow. He says, "Take heart, I have overcome the world." I love that verse and have claimed it in my prayers so many times. "*Lord, you know the trouble and pain I am experiencing, but I thank you that Jesus has overcome the world and all its tribulations. Therefore, I know he will enable me by his Spirit to overcome these situations.*"

It is a prayer that has helped me time and again, and it can help you, too. It is a beautiful promise: "I have overcome the world."

For us to experience the ability to overcome, we must trust God. This means to lean on or lean into. It is a confidence and hope in the refuge of God. Just as the branch leans into the vine, we lean in and stay connected to God through Jesus. Trust is a conscious decision. It is not something you see, but a choice you make. In a Bible concordance, we find more than one hundred references to "trust" or "trustworthy." It is only by trust through tribulation that we will endure and overcome.

Look up the verses listed below or one of your favorites about trust. Find one that speaks to your heart and write it. Claim the verse in your prayers as it applies to your life.

- Proverbs 3:5–6
- Psalm 143:8
- Isaiah 12:2
- Isaiah 26:3–4
- Jeremiah 49:11
- John 14:1
- Hebrews 2:13

Why is this verse meaningful to you?

The message of hope given through Scripture is used to strengthen our faith and trust in God when life is hard. It gives us encouragement when we want to give up on life and give up on Jesus. When we grieve, it is difficult to stand strong in our faith, but it is a critical time to do so. My prayer is that you will continue to trust God with all your heart, mind, soul, and strength.

Jesus prepared the disciples for tribulation by letting them know he is greater and has overcome the world.

Let not your hearts be troubled,
neither let them be afraid.

John 14:27b (ESV)

"Moreover, I have
acquired Ruth the Moabitess,
the widow of Mahlon,
to be my wife."

Ruth 4:10a (NASB95)

Chapter 15

Never Alone

Adrianna Anderson

Keep your life free from love of money,
and be content with what you have, for he has said,
"I will never leave you nor forsake you."
Hebrews 13:5 (ESV)

At twenty-four years of age, I found myself in a place I didn't want to be or ever imagined I would be. I became a widow. This was a new world for me, and I didn't like it. While I am not comfortable sharing the details of the "how," I can share ways God cared for me as a young widow and helped me move forward following the loss of my husband.

There is a Bible verse that says, "Father of the fatherless and protector of widows is God in his holy habitation" (Psa. 68:5 ESV). That is one way God proved his love and care for me—by showing himself as protector in my life in so many ways:

- He protected my mind and spirit when walking through the loss of my first husband.
- He provided a wonderful and strong Christian couple to walk alongside me and provide me with counseling and prayer.
- He continued to provide ways for me to serve him in ministry.

- He continued to grow a love in my heart for him and his Word.

I am so thankful for the amazing opportunity God has given me in ministry. He allowed me to serve as a missionary in a foreign land. While there, I worked in a Christian school where I taught English to fifth and sixth graders. I also could teach ESL classes in the local Hispanic community where I served. Although moving from a secular job in America to a foreign country isn't easy, my family upbringing had already acclimated me to the culture. But it's still never easy to leave all you have known to start something new. On top of all the change I was about to embark upon, I was still walking through grief, and it was difficult. God is constant to remind me, "Adrianna, you are not alone." When I missed the American way of life, he would whisper, "I am with you." When I had to adjust to a different culture and way of life, he would bring me to passages in his Word that spoke to the specific need I had. God works in our lives as widows in so many ways.

Some tangible ways that God provided for me are:

- He provided for all my financial needs as I served him in a foreign country.
- He provided a wonderful church family for me to receive spiritual support and where I could actively serve him in the body of Christ.
- He provided wonderful Christian women friendships that I needed so that I had a community to be a part of.
- He provided times of rest and renewal for me to go back to the States for seasons of sabbatical and time with family and friends.

I use the word "provided" a lot and for many reasons. You see, God speaks about widows in his Word at least eighty times throughout the Old and New Testaments. Why? Because he loves the widow and cares for her. He promises to provide everything she needs. Widows are on his mind and heart such that he issued a mandate to the church to take care of them. The Pentateuch (the first five books of the Bible) also included laws that mandated protection for widows or endure the penalty and consequence of God's judgment for abusing and mistreating them. That's serious!

What I want you to know is that as a widow, God always reminded me I was never alone, even when I felt alone. It took some time for me to believe it, but God was always faithful and patient, showing me he was with me all the time (see Hebrews 13:5).

If you during this season of widowhood feel alone, please consider these things:

- Get in God's Word. There are so many truths he wants to remind you of and speak to you about. Find passages with principles that you can apply in your life in this season.
- If you feel alone, be honest with him about it and cast those cares on him through prayer (see 1 Peter 5:7). Write your prayers in a journal and leave space to write how God answers you (make a note of the date). He will answer you!
- Take care of yourself. Don't neglect your health. It's important to do the things we sometimes take for granted, like getting out in the sun and getting proper nutrition. Remember, you are his temple (see 1 Corinthians 6:19–20)!
- Fear not: Did you know that there are 365 references throughout Scripture that speak to this statement? One for every day of the year. God knows we will always need to be reminded of this, especially in the season we walk through as widows.

You are never alone, dear sister, even if your heart feels otherwise. You are never alone, dear sister, even when you are in a crowded room with familiar faces. You are never alone, dear sister, when it's just you. God sees you and hears you. He longs for fellowship with you, and he is never too busy to listen to you. He is your friend that sticks closer than anyone else (see Proverbs 18:24). He longs to heal your broken heart and is only a whisper away. God is your source, and you are never alone.

Tips for Living Forward

In your loneliest moments, cling to the truth that God is always with you (see Deuteronomy 31:6). Find a faith-based support group and allow others to walk this journey with you. Their support can be a tangible reminder of God's presence.

Message of Hope – 15

Preparation for Eternity

And this is eternal life,
that they know you, the only true God,
and Jesus Christ whom you have sent.

John 17:3 (ESV)

When we understand eternity with Jesus, it helps us to accept the loss of a loved one. But it does not negate the pain of the loss or the grief that follows. That is why reading Scripture each day is important. Even though we may not be able to focus, somehow God uses his Word to penetrate our heart and give us strength and comfort. And it is all because of the sacrifice he made for us through Jesus.

> Read John 17:1–5. What authority did God give Jesus according to verse 2?

> What is eternal life? See verse 3.

Look again at John 14:1–6. This passage gives a clear picture of Jesus's role in our eternity. He prepares a place for us and is the way to get there.

Read Acts 4:11–12. What does Peter say about Jesus?

Now read Romans 10:13. Write the verse here.

To be saved is the assurance of eternity in heaven. I'm sure this is not new news to you, but reading Scripture about it strengthens our faith and gives comfort regarding those who have gone before us.

In the first five verses of John 17, we read about the glory of God and Jesus's prayer to the Father for his own glory. He concluded this section with the words in verse 5, "And now, Father, glorify me in your own presence with the glory that I had with you before the world existed" (ESV).

Think about that statement. Jesus's prayer shows us he was with the Father before the world existed. When we get to heaven, we will see Jesus in all his glory! Immediately after that power statement, he began to pray for those who follow him.

- When you were caregiving, he was praying for you.
- When you were in the moments of death and loss, he was praying for you.
- When you went through the funeral, he was praying for you.
- In your grief, he prays for you.
- And now, in this new beginning, he prays for you. All by the power of the Holy Spirit who intercedes on our behalf when we cannot pray for ourselves.

Jesus prepared the disciples for eternity by his prayers.

"Arise, go to Zarephath,
which belongs to Sidon,
and dwell there.
Behold, I have commanded a
widow there to feed you."

1 Kings 17:9 (ESV)

Chapter 16

In Flight

Sandy Weiss

For your Maker is your husband.

Isa. 54:5 (NIV)

Thirty years to the day that our family landed in Nairobi, Kenya (East Africa), to serve as missionaries, my husband, Lee, suffered a massive stroke in our kitchen. Following his hospitalization, we brought Lee home with around-the-clock care by two male nurses and the loving attention of our daughter, Sarah, and son-in-law, Victor. Four and a half months later, my eighty-year-old husband slipped into God's eternal presence in our living room in Nairobi. Because of his great suffering, Lee's passing was comforting in a way. I knew he was now healthy and happy, and I would join him one glorious day. But I also experienced loneliness.

A month after Lee died, God in his mercy gave me these words from Isaiah 54:5 (NIV): "For your Maker is your husband— the Lord Almighty is his name—the Holy One of Israel is your Redeemer; he is called the God of all the earth." This became the bedrock of my new life as a widow. It still sustains me every day. There are times I feel like a worm crawling along in life, trying to find the new me. This isolation increased during COVID-19 after I sold my car. Normal active daily life around the world came to a standstill. BUT GOD ... Little did I realize the new way I would "fly" around Nairobi—THANK GOD FOR UBER! I started praying for God to send the drivers of his choice and to guide me if I was to speak to them. I never expected a new ministry. God gave me new wings to write and share Bible brochures. Several of my drivers received Jesus as their personal Savior! One even prayed while he was driving me home from the store. We still keep in touch two years later! Sometimes, I feel like a caterpillar that has crawled into a cocoon—quiet and alone. From the outside, it may look like not much is happening—even boring. I have learned it is healthy to acknowledge difficulties, but not to keep my focus on them. I don't want my problems to become idols by making them bigger than God.

My hands remind me of people I can pray for. I use them as a handy reminder to connect my Maker Husband with others to fulfill God's purpose.

- I hold my hand in front of me with my thumb pointing toward me.
- My THUMB is nearest to me and represents: 1 = Myself and My Family
- My FOREFINGER represents those closest in my heart and those I see often: 2 = My Friends, Neighbors, and Enemies
- My MIDDLE FINGER, the tallest, represents: 3 = My Church, Ministries, and Missions
- My RING FINGER represents: 4 = My Nation
- My SMALLEST FINGER reminds me of places far away from me and the needy: 5 = Other Places; Those in Weakness

As I look to my Maker Husband in my cocoon, he is transforming me. I am learning along with Paul, who wrote while suffering in prison, to give thanks in everything, while not FOR everything. I am learning to SEE GOD BIGGER through every difficulty I face. When I become anxious or worried, I am learning to ask, even out loud, "God, are you worried about this?" Then I remember God has zero worries and says 365 times in the Bible not to fear. So, I recall, "Your Word tells me not to be anxious about anything, but IN EVERYTHING, by prayer and petition WITH THANKSGIVING, to make my requests known to you." And I ask God to give me his supernatural peace.

As I keep SEEING GOD BIGGER, two wings I enjoy daily in greater ways are God's Word and gratitude.

(1) **God's Word** gives me confidence because it is true, never changes, and will last forever. I have discovered that paraphrasing Scripture can give hope and be very healing. Recently, I personalized Psalm 23 for me as a widow. It brought me great comfort.

> Lord, you are my Husband; I shall not be in want. You give me rest places. You refresh me. You renew me inside to help me keep going. You are giving me the right direction for the future. Even though my loved one is gone, I will not fear because I know you are by my side. You give me courage and comfort because you guide and protect me, for your honor. You nourish me even in hard times and places. You elevate and energize my thinking and outlook. You satisfy me in abundance. You not only go before me and are with me, but you also follow me all the time. Someday I will reach your place, and it will be heavenly, because we are together and never to be separated.

(2) **Gratitude** frees me to fly higher. Each day I wake up filled with thankfulness for simple joys: getting dressed, looking good for my Maker Husband, the surrounding beauty, delicious meals, kind Uber drivers, and so much more. The forty-four years I had with Lee Weiss as my husband are reasons to be thankful. I am

also grateful for this season of widowhood that is drawing me closer to my Maker, my Husband.

Those words from Isaiah 41:13–14 (NIV) about the biblical worm fill me with gratitude:

> *"For I am the LORD, your God, who takes hold of your right hand and says to you, do not fear; I will help you. Do not be afraid, you worm Jacob, little Israel, do not fear, for I myself will help you," declares the LORD, your Redeemer, the Holy One of Israel.*

Because I have received Jesus as my personal Savior from sin and am growing in living for his glory, I am being transformed from a God-valued lowly worm crawling on this planet and given wings to fly now and in a Happy Forever After beyond my wildest imagination. My heart sings to think of winging our way through the heavens together.

Tips for Living Forward

When grieving, it is difficult to be joyful or thankful. But making a list of what we are thankful for redirects our focus and uplifts our spirit. For example, I am thankful to be the bride of Christ.

Throughout the Old Testament, God refers to His chosen people, the nation of Israel, as His bride. In Isaiah 54:5, He tells Israel, "Your Maker is your husband—the LORD Almighty is His name." In the New Testament, Jesus refers to Himself as the Bridegroom and to His church as His bride.

– Cindi McMenamin
When Women Walk Alone,
©2012, Harvest House Publishers

Message of Hope – 16

Preparation for Prayer

...he lifted up his eyes to heaven...
John 17:1a (ESV)

You may be familiar with Matthew 6:8–13 where Jesus taught the disciples how to pray. The prayer included worship of God and asking for God's will, provision, forgiveness, guidance, and deliverance. Now in John 17, we read the great priestly prayer of Jesus for those who follow him. This includes you and me. It is a beautiful prayer.

> **Read all of John 17. What part of this prayer speaks to you in a personal way?**

> **Read Acts 1:6–11. What event is taking place?**

> Continue reading with verses 12–14. At this point, Jesus had died and was buried, but he rose again and appeared to the disciples. Then he departed for heaven. After this, what is the first thing they did?

> What did they learn from Jesus that they put into practice according to verse 14?

The church is built on the cornerstone of Jesus with the disciples as the foundation he laid. The gospel message of Christ has continued through all generations beginning with the cornerstone. The building structures of that day were made with stone. The cornerstone was laid first, then other stones were placed to form the foundation. It was the guide of the foundation so the walls built upon it would be straight. Jesus used this language of what was familiar to the disciples so they would understand the order of the gospel to be carried into the future.

Jesus is not only the first stone upon which the foundation of our faith is laid, but he is also the last stone, placed upon completion. He is the Alpha and Omega, the beginning and end. When we trust him fully, we will not stumble and fall. He is able to carry the weight of our grief and burdens without crumbling under the pressure.

Just as the walls of a structure are built upon a solid foundation with a cornerstone that will not crumble, we are like walls. Our faith is built upon the foundation guided by the cornerstone that withstands our heavy load. Take it to Jesus in prayer, every day, any time.

> Look back at Jesus's prayer in John 17. Just to solidify in our minds who Jesus prayed for, write verse 9.

> Now go to Romans 8:26–27. How does Jesus pray for you and me today?

Jesus prepared the disciples for prayer by praying for them. His Spirit intercedes for us now. Take comfort in knowing that even when we are so wrapped up in our pain and grief and can't pray, Jesus prays for us by his Spirit.

Cast your burden on the Lord,
and he will sustain you;
he will never permit
the righteous to be moved.
Psalm 55:22 (ESV)

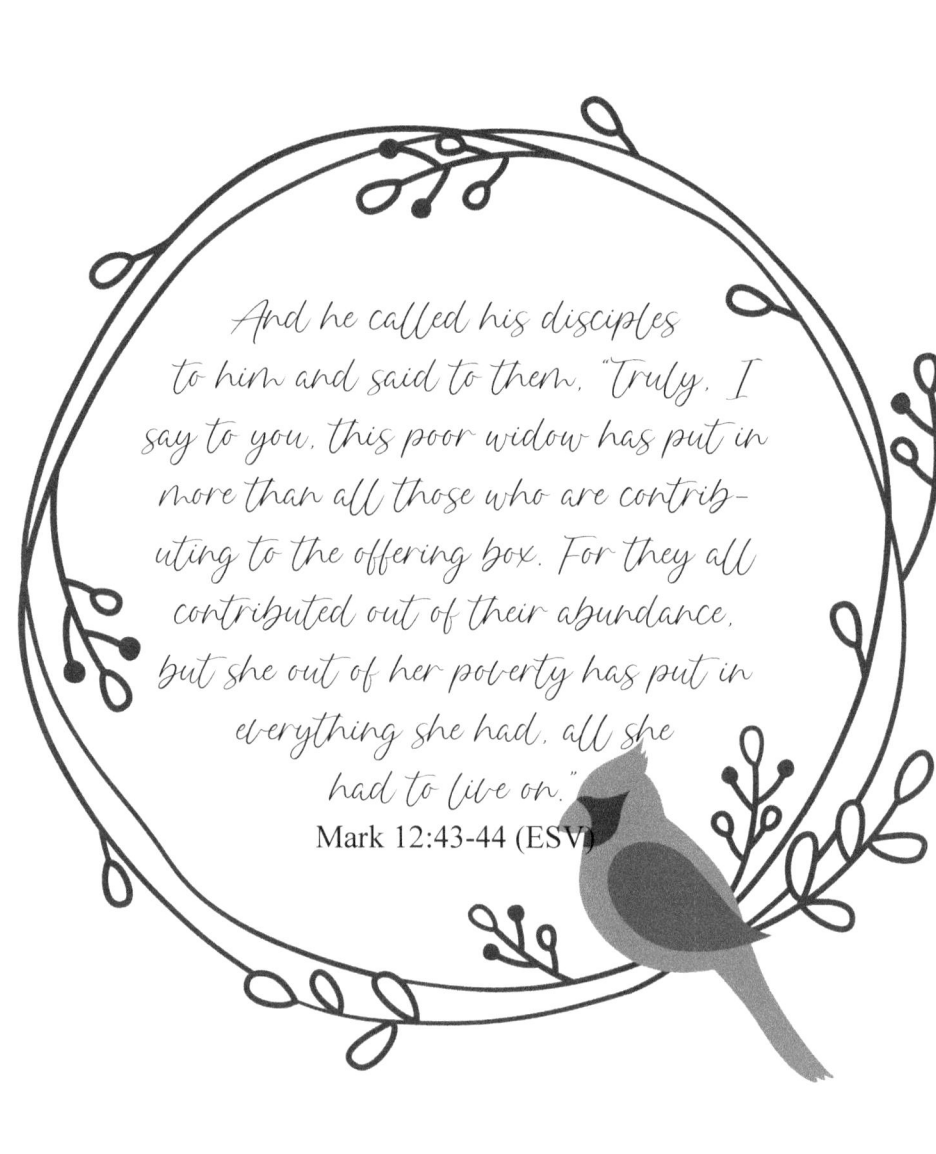

And he called his disciples
to him and said to them, "Truly, I
say to you, this poor widow has put in
more than all those who are contrib-
uting to the offering box. For they all
contributed out of their abundance,
but she out of her poverty has put in
everything she had, all she
had to live on."

Mark 12:43-44 (ESV)

Chapter 17

The Unwanted Detour

Kathy Harris

Because of the Lord's great love we are not consumed,
for his compassions never fail.

Lamentations 3:22 (NIV)

At a very young age, I knew I wanted to be a wife, a mom, and a writer of books.

First came college and, after graduation, a job in marketing—not quite a writer, but the dream was still intact. I was in my mid-thirties when I met my soulmate—a word that gets tossed around a lot. But when you know, you know. And he was all that.

I have always said we had been looking for each other for years. And when it happened, it happened quickly. Two years later we were married. Without a doubt, God brought us together for better and for worse, and in sickness and in health. There were amazing times, and there were hard times. But we loved through it all.

The most difficult thing we had to face was his health problems. Two years after we were married, he had his first heart attack. He was only forty-two years old. At the time, we were in the process of trying to adopt a child.

Almost everything changed with that hospital stay. For weeks, we didn't know if he would live or die. When he returned home, his personality was different. His fears were different. He used to say that young people think they are six feet tall and bulletproof, and he no longer felt bulletproof.

We navigated through the next two years, finally getting back to where we started. Perhaps even stronger than we were. He was whole, even if a little patched up. The heart bypass he received would get him through the next nineteen years. But those first two years of healing had taken its toll on our plans to adopt. And even though being a mom was no longer a possibility for me, I was grateful I still had my husband to share life with.

In a world filled with rust and ruin, marriage is one of the things we expect to last forever. No matter how young or how old we are when we marry, we think about the time we will have together. We make plans. We set goals. We envision ourselves as that cute older couple walking hand in hand into the sunset.

And, I still had one big goal—to become a published novelist. Having your family's support is important to any writer's success. When you're on deadline, nothing else matters. Not housework, not cooking extravagant meals, and often not sleep. But my husband was all in.

When I wanted to quit, his encouragement kept me going. When I attended writers' conferences to pitch my manuscript, he would soothe my fears—and calm my nerves—from the other end of the phone. When my confidence failed, and it inevitably did, I relied on his. Finally, together, we celebrated the release of my first novel. He went with me to out-of-state book signings and to a conference to receive an award. My success was truly our success. I can't imagine doing it without him.

I was working on my second book when he died. His heart problems returned with a vengeance, and one thing led to another. He fought with everything he had, but it wasn't enough this time.

I had written about detours on my author blog for years, but I wasn't prepared for this one. Losing a spouse is one of the most unwelcome detours we can face. And, ironically, it's one we must walk alone. But even our unwanted detours can be a part of God's plan. He can use the pain in our lives to fully speak to us. Or, perhaps, more accurately, to engage our listening ear.

C. S. Lewis said it this way: "God whispers to us in our pleasures, speaks in our conscience, but shouts in our pain: it is His megaphone to rouse a deaf world."[5]

Life after loss hasn't been easy. But since that time, I have heard God's voice, and felt his presence, in supernatural ways. And, eventually, my pain was turned into praise. Praise for the almost three decades of life my husband and I shared.

Looking back, I can see God's hand, his miracles, and his mercies in our time together, and I am grateful for those extra years he gave us after that first heart attack. It was, perhaps, the greatest detour of all. We were tried by fire, but because of God's love, we were not consumed.

Eventually, I was able to get back to writing again. And my late husband's encouragement continues to keep me motivated. My time with him, and my time afterward as a caregiver to my parents, provided great insight. A deeper understanding of life and love. And a greater dependence on God, not only as my Savior but as my Shepherd and my greatest source of strength.

I'm not sure who said it first, but I've heard it said that God often uses our deepest pain as the launching pad for our greatest calling. He did in my life.

How about you?

Tips for Living Forward

Only God knows what is next for us. Trusting him helps us to accept that he knows best, and by accepting, we are okay with where he leads. Bible Study and prayer increase our faith and trust.

---

5   Lewis, C. S. *The Problem of Pain* (New York, Macmillan Company, 1944).

Message of Hope – 17

Preparation for Sanctification

Sanctify them in the truth;
your word is truth.

John 17:17 (ESV)

Let's face it. We are human beings with flaws. Not one of us is perfect because of the sin nature of Adam. That is why God sent his Son to make a way for us to be forgiven. Therefore, our human nature is sometimes at war with our spirit. We need a constant awareness of the lifelong process of sanctification. It is a growth process leading toward spiritual maturity. This occurs as we seek truth from God's Word to deepen our relationship with him through Jesus. Daily prayer and Bible study is how we learn how to live out our faith. To be sanctified is to be set apart. It is the ongoing work of the Holy Spirit within us.

> **In Jesus's prayer, he asked God to sanctify his people in truth. His Word is truth. What does John 1:1 say about the Word?**

The apostle Paul followed the example of Jesus in his prayer. Read 1 Thessalonians 5:23–24. Paul is praying for the believers. How is God identified and for what does Paul pray?

What does the process of being sanctified do for us? Look up the word "blameless" in a dictionary and write the definition.

> In the Bible, a blameless person is one who is faithful to God and cannot be accused of wrongdoing. Read Psalm 15:2 and 18:23.

To be blameless is to take on the character of Christ. It is a moral character to be achieved by sanctification and is not something earned. It is imputed by the death and resurrection of Christ (see Colossians 1:22).

The characteristic of blamelessness should define the believer's private and public life as a reflection of the transforming work of God's grace in salvation. Jesus prayed it for his followers and God is faithful to do it. The ongoing work of the Holy Spirit in our lives continues until we reach heaven.

> Jesus's prayer in John 17:18–19 establishes that his followers can be sanctified because he consecrated himself for our sake. How is it affirmed in verse 20 that this prayer includes you and me?

You may be asking, what does this have to do with me as a widow? How does this help me? The answer is the closer we draw to Jesus, and the deeper our relationship with him, we become stronger, gain peace, and are motivated and inspired to live according to God's plan and will for our future.

Jesus prepared his followers for how to be set apart from the world and all its woes, and to live by his truth. By doing so, there will be peace in our hearts.

*Honor widows
who are widows indeed;*
1 Timothy 5:3 (NASB95)

Chapter 18

A Light Turned On

Virginia Grounds

He dawns on them like the morning light,
like the sun shining forth on a cloudless morning,
like rain that makes grass sprout from the earth.

2 Samuel 23:4 (ESV)

It seemed like an internal switch flipped. I cannot explain it, but after a time of living in a mental fog, the light finally shone through. Grief is like that. We want to take a step forward, but it is too foggy to see. The timing of light shining through is different for everyone. But God times our way back into the light to meet our individual situation and needs.

For me, once that happened, I sensed a stirring in my spirit to let go of a job providing financial support and get back to my call to ministry. The job was consuming my time and leaving me depleted. I wrestled with the decision for months. Those people were there for me after losing my husband. I had no reason to leave except that God led me in that direction.

After months of struggle, I let go. My last day was on a Wednesday. Less than four days later, on Monday, I received a text message from a friend asking if I would be interested in a job with her company. I agreed to meet with them and became excited as I heard what my role was to entail. God was moving me forward, just not in the way I planned. I wanted to move closer to family that lived ten hours away from me. Even though it was what I wanted, God said, "Not now."

It is difficult to go where God leads us when we want something different. And yet, when the text came, I knew what I was to do. It was a new beginning, a new opportunity.

This is the encouragement I want to give in this story. The hope for all of us is that even when we think God is silent and not answering our prayers, he is waiting for us to pay attention and do what he asks of us. He doesn't want us to get stuck in grief. God's work in our lives on earth will not end until we leave it. The key is to allow ourselves to grieve for a season so we can heal. Then pray, asking God to take away our mental fog and help us know what is next in our lives. The door he opens may be far from anything we would have thought.

The apostle Paul wrote to the saints at Philippi to forget those things behind and press on to the upward call of God in Christ Jesus. I know he is speaking of the sin that entangled us before we believed in the Lord. But as it applies to us, it doesn't mean we are to forget our loved one. It is the precious memories of them we will hold on to. I believe as it applies to our widowhood, we can forget the pain of loss in a way that does not hold us forever in its grip.

Then we can know when God is stirring up something within us. We can chase the darkness away with the light of his love. When we recognize that he's nudging us from one season to the next and we respond, doors are open to move forward. Our lives don't end just because we are alone without our husbands.

We are not alone on this journey. We have traveled through a winter season of heartache. But the good thing about winter is that it is followed by spring with new beginnings as we plant seeds of hope in our hearts and see new opportunities arise.

So often we may think we are ready for something, but we are not. I thought I was ready to move, but looking back, I realized I was not. Grief still held me in its grip. Getting ready means spending time with the Lord each day in prayer and reading the Bible. There will be days when we have it open on our lap, and nothing penetrates our mind. But if we keep putting God's Word in front of us daily, asking him to remove our mental fog and heal our brain, soon our minds will clear, and we can get ready for his plan.

We're still able to experience joy, laughter, and thought. In God's time, we will overcome the dark cloud of grief while still holding onto our love and memories of our husband, and without feeling guilty. But it takes patience as we wait for God to stir something in us to answer the question of what's next.

Has Jesus come through for you in your loss and grief? How can we get through the difficulties after the loss of our husband without Jesus? He gives comfort in our sorrow. He is our ever-present help in times of trouble. In our despair, he lifts us up and places peace and hope within our heart. When we have regrets, he replaces our guilt with reassurance of love. When we are stuck in despair, he does not leave us but rather helps us to focus on those things that are good and positive with a good result.

God is our refuge and strength,
a very present help in trouble.

Psalm 46:1 (KJV)

Tips for Living Forward

Trust is a choice, even when it feels difficult. Proverbs 3:5–6 reminds us to lean not on our understanding but on God's wisdom. Surrender each day to him, knowing his plans are for your good.

Message of Hope – 18

Preparation for Unity

I in them and you in me,
that they may become perfectly one...
John 17:23a (ESV)

It is not uncommon for disharmony to occur in our lives. Perhaps in marriage, in our work or community—even in church. But that is not what Jesus prayed for us. He prayed for unity. I regret the times in our marriage when we were not united on a decision, or when we argued. It is one of those things I wish I had a do-over. If someone reading this is in the caregiving stage, my best advice is to have no regrets. Give love in all you say in do.

In this imperfect world, unity doesn't seem possible. Yet it can be done by the grace of God. It is to be joined together as a whole and have love amongst believers. We not only need unity in our personal lives, but in our churches, now more than ever. The prime example of perfect unity is in God the Father, Jesus the Son, and the Holy Spirit—the three-in-one holy trinity.

Therefore, let's take a look at how unity can take place. In the time of Jesus on earth, there was much disunity among the people who were troubled by opposition regarding religion. There was also division in ethnic and cultural groups. How interesting that after all these years, we still see this in our world now. Division continues to be a spiritual and cultural problem.

> **Read John 17:11, 23. Why is Jesus praying that God will keep believers in his name? How can this happen?**

> Look at verse 26. Jesus made God known to us. What deep emotion does he desire for us?

It is only by the love of God that we will be able to reach the state of unity that Jesus prayed for. He loves us with an everlasting love. The final verses of his prayer are for unity and love. They go hand in hand.

You may have someone in your family or group of friends that does not understand your emotional state and why you haven't gotten past your grief. This causes hurt feelings, possible criticism, and loss of relationships. But asking God to love that person through you is a way to get beyond the separation and back to unity in the family, work, and church. And now may the God of all comfort give you comfort that you may be able to comfort others as one in Christ as you take to heart and practice living according to the preparations provided by Jesus for those who follow him. It won't bring back our loved ones, but it will give us peace, purpose, and a plan for what's next.

Blessed be the God and Father of our Lord Jesus Christ, the Father of mercies and God of all comfort, who comforts us in all our affliction, so that we may be able to comfort those who are in any affliction, with the comfort with which we ourselves are comforted by God.

2 Corinthians 1:3–4 (ESV)

CONCLUSION

Hope Is Future-Focused

Storing up for themselves the treasure
of a good foundation for the future,
so that they may take hold of that which is truly life.

1 Timothy 6:19 (NASB)

Hope is always looking ahead. We can face our future with a confident expectation of something good. It is moving toward the invisible, anticipating an excellent result. Some may say, "But I have no hope. Distress fills my life now. How can I expect a better future?"

To respond to that question, read what the Bible says about the future. We begin by looking at the life of the prophet Jeremiah, a man who suffered from the actions of others. Because Jeremiah obeyed God's call in his life, people rejected him, threatened to murder him, and persecuted him. Jeremiah is often called the "weeping prophet" because he mourned the fact that the people of the city of Judah refused to heed God's Word, and Jerusalem lay in ruins.

Jeremiah understood the pain and grief of suffering, and yet his faith and hope in God gave him the courage to press on during it all. He kept his mind fixed on the future. Jeremiah had hope!

We may work all our lives looking forward to retirement with our spouse. But when they die before we do, the hopes and dreams we had together disappeared. Yet, according to 1 Timothy 6:19, the foundation for retirement is in doing good works, being generous, and sharing the faith God has entrusted to us.

Can you relate to Jeremiah's suffering? A time when you were doing what the Lord asked of you and suffered for it? In a situation like Jeremiah's, what is a typical human response—to give up or press on? Though we've dedicated our lives to ministry, we're not exempt from suffering, as Jeremiah shows. But we can have hope as we continue to do the work God places before us.

God says when we pray, he will listen, and when we search for him with all our heart, we will find him. And if we do not pray as we should, he promises that for those who love and follow him, his Spirit will intercede on our behalf.

God's Word and work are a source of joy and contentment for me. Hope is the confident expectation of something good. Good is Jesus and our eternity with him. God has promised good to those who love him, and that promise is our hope.

He is our God of hope.

Tips for Family and Friends of a Widow

It's awkward—that visit to a friend who lost a spouse. You don't know what to say or do. You want to help and so you ask, "What can I do?" The problem with asking that question is the new widow doesn't know her need at that moment. But know this—she has needs. She'll hold back, unsure if she should share her needs when she realizes she needs help. Time passes, and others have forgotten to ask again.

Everything is different now for the widow. The tasks her husband used to do around the house remain undone. Her responsibilities are double. The words of comfort are gone, and she's left alone to face the crushing weight of exhaustion. She is no longer a couple but doesn't feel single. She feels lost and alone. Pray for your friend.

From what I, and others before me, have experienced in the death of our husbands, here are a few practical tips to help you know what to do or say to someone in this new position.

1. Your friend may not be tall enough to change a light bulb, or strong enough to carry a ladder inside to do so. Offer to do the little things like that, even lifting heavy objects.

2. Does the recent widow have family nearby? If not, she will isolate herself in grief. She needs a friend during this time. Call to check on her often. When she wants to get out, invite her somewhere fun or spiritually enriching. I think of Naomi and Ruth when Naomi just wanted to be left alone. But Ruth, a recent widow herself, stayed by her side through many hardships.

3. Is the trash dumpster close by, or does she need to go a distance to take the trash? If you live close to her, offer to take her trash when you take yours.

4. Be a listening ear when she is ready to talk about her loved one. There may be those who wonder why he is all she talks about and question why she doesn't move on. Please don't

be that kind of friend by changing the subject each time she talks about him. Memories are all she has at this point.

5. What about taxes? If her husband always took care of taxes and their financials, she may need someone who has experience with those things to help her on a volunteer basis.

6. Driving may be a challenge for the widow. Offer to drive her wherever she needs to go.

7. She will need to contact the social security office. It may be overwhelming. How can you help with that?

8. The Bible tells the church and family to take care of a widow with provisions. It is first the responsibility of family of a widow. If she has no family support, then the church is to help her.

These are only a few of many suggestions and may not be the need of every widow. Be a friend who sticks closer than a brother or sister and you will see her needs and know how to help.

Then they lifted up their voices and wept again.
And Orpah kissed her mother-in-law, but Ruth clung to her.

Ruth 1:14 (ESV)

Contributing Authors

(Listed alphabetically)

ADAMS, Susie Kinslow – Susie is a gifted author, writer, speaker, and storyteller. For forty-two years, she worked alongside her husband, Dr. Russell Adams, as he served as director of missions in Missouri and pastored in California, Oklahoma, and Missouri. Susie led women's Bible studies and directed women's retreats in California, Oklahoma, and Missouri. She is an active member of Springfield Writer's Guild and Christian Writers. Her books are: My Mother My Child (a practical guide dealing with Alzheimer's and elderly parents); The Rebel and Preacher Man (a memoir); and Patches Farmland Adventures and Patches Joyland Express (children's coloring/activity books) (available on Amazon). Susie also served as a women's ministry director for twenty-three years. More information and an encouraging blog is available at www.susiekinslowadams.com.

ANDERSON, Adrianna – Adrianna is a Bible teacher, speaker, writer, Lifeway women trainer, and Lifeway women event specialist. She is the director of the Ministry Wives Network for the Missouri Baptist Convention. She teaches and speaks on widowhood, prayer, mental health, apologetics, and racial unity from a biblical perspective. Adrianna holds a master's degree in biblical studies, is a graduate of New Orleans Baptist Theological Seminary, and is working on doctoral studies in public theology. She is a runner, an avid book reader, and a tea connoisseur who loves reading God's Word. You can reach her at avanderson@me.com.

EIDSON, Loretta – Award-winning author Loretta Eidson loves writing romantic suspense. She believes in the power of prayer and enjoys putting her characters in realistic situations where they must trust God to pull them through. Loretta is an AWSA certified coach and is represented by Tamela Hancock Murray. She is published by Harlequin's Love Inspired Suspense. She can be reached at www.lorettaeidson.com.

ENGRAM, Sharon – Sharon is a national and international speaker and co-author of Surviving Widowhood: 40 Devotions of Hope. She loves teaching God's Word, and mentoring and inspiring women to discover how to know God deeper. Sharon has traveled to fifty-five countries. She was joyfully married to her late husband and best friend for sixty years, actively serving alongside him in the three churches he pastored. Sharon is a grateful mom of four adult children, fourteen grandchildren, and ten great-grandchildren.

FINN, Virgie Mae – Virgie Mae, age eighty-two, was born in Tennessee Ridge and now lives in St. Louis, Missouri. She is a widowed mother of two boys and one girl, grandmother to nine, great-grandmother to eight, and expecting two more greats this year. Her passion is living out GOD's purpose for her life, family, and friends.

GROUNDS, Virginia – Virginia is an author, speaker, certified professional publisher, and hospice chaplain. She has years of experience teaching Bible study in her home church and at women's events. She served with her late husband for twenty years in full-time ministry to people in crisis. Her recent books are Guide to Deeper Prayer and Ricky the Racecar, a children's book. She is a member of CIPA and AWSA writer associations. She can be reached at www.virginiagrounds.net, www.hope4widows.com and www.breakthroughchristianpublishing.com.

HARRIS, Kathy – Kathy is an author by way of a "divine detour" into the Nashville entertainment business. After graduating with a communications degree from Southern Illinois University, she moved to Tennessee to work in the Christian music industry. That position soon transitioned into what would become a long-tenured country music marketing career. In 2007, Kathy sold her first Christian non-fiction story. Abingdon Press published her debut novel, The Road to Mercy, in 2012. Iron Stream Media released Deadly Commitment, Deadly Connection, and Deadly Conclusion, her three-book romantic suspense series, in 2019–2023. She is currently working on her next series. Follow Kathy on Facebook, Twitter, and Instagram. Read her Divine Detour blog at www.divinedetour.com and check out her books at www. kathyharrisbooks.com.

HARRIS, Paulette – Paulette is a published author of novels, short stories, devotionals, poems, and her favorite form of writing—scripts. She has been a widow for two years. Her church, family, author, and movie-guide friends have been a tremendous support as she embraces her call to continue on until the Lord summons her home. She lives in Tennessee with a Ragdoll cat who has agreed to let her live with him—Sunny, a precious and loyal friend who along with Jesus loves her unconditionally. You can reach her at www.pauletteharris.com.

JOHNS, Kaye – Kaye is an author, speaker, co-founder of Tandem Prayer, and Director of Prayer at e3 Partners. Kaye produced a daily prayer radio feature on a Christian radio station in Dallas (KCBI) for twenty years. She and her late husband wrote and published a wide selection of materials on prayer—including Scripture prayer guides, prayer journals, and two video-based prayer studies for individuals and small groups: *Praying to Make a Difference* and *How to Have a Quiet Time in a Busy World.* These studies have been used by more than 3,500 churches in America, helping people to deepen their prayer lives and have a more meaningful relationship with Jesus Christ. Their books, *Higher Ground, Deeper Truth,* and *Prayers for the Moment,* were published by B&H Publishing. They have written an unsurpassed library of prayer resources and videos. You can find Kaye's messages and videos on prayer for free at www. tandemprayer.org.

JONES, Louise Tucker – Louise is a speaker, columnist, and author/co-author of six books, including the Gold Medallion award-winning book *Extraordinary Kids.* Her poignant life stories have been published in hundreds of magazines and numerous anthologies, including over a dozen *Chicken Soup for the Soul* titles. Married to her college sweetheart for forty-five years before he relocated to heaven, Louise is a mother, grandmother, professed chocoholic, and founder of the support group, Wives with Heavenly Husbands. Find her at LouiseTJ@cox.net and www. LouiseTuckerJones.com.

KAUSEN, Kelly – Kelly attended Biola University and started her business career in advertising sales for newspapers, radio, and then television. Later, she was the publisher of a local magazine and then newspaper. She started a local charity called Helping Others More Efficiently with the acronym HOME and was awarded a Leadership Award by the local ABC affiliate in San Diego.

LEAVITT, Jenny – Jenny is an award-winning author, speaker, and grief recovery coach dedicated to helping others navigate the pain of loss and rediscover hope through faith. As a mother who tragically lost her seventeen-year-old son, Jacob, in 2015 to a drunk driver, Jenny understands the depth of grief and the challenges of finding healing. She draws from her own journey, along with her expertise as a board-certified master mental health coach specializing in grief, loss, and trauma-informed care, to provide practical, Christ-centered resources and support. Jenny offers online courses, including, "Resilient: How to Navigate Grief While Holding onto Your Hope in Christ." Learn more about her work at www.jenny-leavitt.com and www.resilienthope.net.

PASOUR, Katherine – Katherine is an author, speaker, farmer, and a veteran teacher of over forty years. She blogs weekly at https://katherinepasour.com with a focus on faith, wellness, service, and the lessons nature teaches. She is a regular contributor to *Refresh Bible Study Magazine*, published by Lighthouse Bible Studies. Katherine has books published by Morgan James: *Faith*, a wellness devotional/Bible study; *Honoring God with My Body: Journey to Wellness and a Healthy Lifestyle;* and *Stay the Course: A Devotional Handbook to Survive and Thrive in Your First Year of College (and Beyond)*. You can connect with Katherine on her website (see above), Facebook https://www.facebook.com/katherine-pasourauthor, X (Twitter) https://x.com/KatherinePasour, and Instagram https://www.instagram.com/katherinepasourauthor/.

ROHLINGER, Lori – Lori was active alongside her late husband, Greg, in founding Palm Valley Church in Arizona, seeing growth to over four thousand worshipers. The couple was an inspiring speaking team—he at the 2013 C3 conference for pastors in Dallas, and she at JustOne virtual conference in 2014 and 2016. Lori also spoke at the in-person Flourish Conference in 2017. She is the mother of three young adult sons and one daughter. She loves breeding her darling Berne doodles while continuing to write and does a weekly podcast, *Beautifully Broken*, about her Christian life. Learn more at https://lorirohlinger.blogspot.com.

TURNER, Sheryl Giesbrecht – Exchanging hurt for hope is Sheryl's focus. She is a recovered drug addict, stage IV cancer survivor, and former widow. She loves to actively apply God's Word as she cares for the overlooked, abandoned, and brokenhearted. She is founder and president of her non-profit, From Ashes to Beauty Inc., and The Widow Project, sponsoring widows in the USA and Africa. An award-winning author of five books, hundreds of her columns and magazine and devotional articles have appeared in *Focus on the Family Magazine*, *Just Between Us*, *The Discipleship Journal*, Walk Thru the Bible's *Indeed* devotions, and Tapestry Press publications. The joys of Sheryl's life are her children and fourteen grandchildren. She is excited about her ten-year marriage to Dr. Jim Turner and their red standard poodles, Sorrel and Sasha. Sheryl holds a Bachelor of Arts from Biola University, a master's in theological counseling, and a Doctor of Divinity degree. She lives in California's central valley where she enjoys running 5K races with her ninety-two-year-old mother. She can be reached at www.sherylgt.com.

WEISS, Sandy – Sandy has led a rich life as a teacher, pastor's wife, mother of five children, and missionary to Africa. She served as a prayer coordinator for Africa Youth for Christ. Sandy co-founded a discipleship ministry, Transformation Ministries Africa, with her late husband, Reverend Lee Weiss, her daughter Sarah, and her husband, Reverend Victor Kabutha. She has also written manuals on prayer and for Women of Worth. She enjoys creating Bible-reading plans and biblically-based brochures and bookmarks. Her heart is to keep on going, growing, and glowing for the glory of God until she meets him face to face.

WHITING, Karen – Karen is an author, speaker, and an experienced survivor of caregiving and natural disasters. Life challenges include category four hurricanes, four lightning strikes to her homes, an earthquake, hailstorm, a derecho (straight-line wind storm), and spontaneous combustible fires in homes where she has lived around the country. She writes to share God's heart messages for women and their families. She is a mom of five and a grandmother. Her spouse passed away from breast cancer. Check out her thirty-four books, especially *Growing a Peaceful Heart* and *Growing a Joyful Heart* as you navigate widowhood and other unexpected challenges. You can contact her at www.karenwhiting.com.

Connect With Me

If this book was helpful to you, will you help me spread the word? There are several ways you can help me get the word out about the message of this book:

- Post a 5-star review on Amazon.
- Write about the book on your social media accounts.
- If you blog, consider referencing the book, or publishing an excerpt from the book with a link back to my website. You have my permission to do this if you provide proper credit and backlinks.
- If you have a podcast, consider having me for an interview about the book.
- Recommend the book to family and friends.
- Purchase additional copies to give away.

You can connect with me at
www.virginiagrounds.net or www.hope4widows.com.

If you have a book in your heart that needs
to be written and published, I can help at
www.breakthroughchristianpublishing.com

Other books by Virginia Grounds available on Amazon.com:
- *Guide to Deeper Prayer*
- *Ricky the Racecar* (children's book)
- *Rock Solid Trust: Trusting God When Life is Hard*

www.ingramcontent.com/pod-product-compliance
Lightning Source LLC
Chambersburg PA
CBHW051626120626
46551CB00014B/1958